The Essential Guide to
Flatsharing

D0865963

The Essential Guide to
Flatsharing

For sharers, lodgers and everyone renting out a room

Rupert Hunt
(founder of SpareRoom.co.uk) and
Matt Hutchinson

howtobooks

Published by How To Books Ltd
Spring Hill House, Spring Hill Road
Begbroke, Oxford OX5 1RX
Tel: (01865) 375794. Fax: (01865) 379162
info@howtobooks.co.uk
www.howtobooks.co.uk

How To Books greatly reduce the carbon footprint of their books by sourcing
their typesetting and printing in the UK.

British Library Cataloguing in Publication Data
A catalogue record for this book is available from the British Library

ISBN: 978 1 84528 484 8

First edition 2009
Second edition 2011

Produced for How To Books by Deer Park Productions, Tavistock
Typeset by Kestrel Data, Exeter
Printed and bound in Great Britain by Bell & Bain Ltd, Glasgow

Contents

Preface
The death of the largest ad site in the world   ix

How to Use this Book   xiii
Read it straight through   xiii
Chapters of interest   xiii
Index   xiv

Introduction: Flatsharing – The Basics (SH/RS/LIL)   1
What is flatsharing?   1
Why flatshare?   1
Who lives in flatshares?   3

Chapter 1: Types of Let (SH/RS)   5
Flat or house share   5
Rooms for rent (live-in landlord)   7
Rooms for rent (live-out landlord)   9
Bedsits   10
Room shares   11
Mon–Fri lets   12
A few thoughts on sublets   13

Chapter 2: Find a Flatshare (RS)   15
Budget   15
What to look for   16
Where to look   26
How to look   27
Professional house shares   29
Viewings   30
Setting up your own flatshare   33

Chapter 3: Find a Flatmate (SH/LIL)   34
Who do you want to live with?   34
Where to look   38
How to look   43
Viewings and interviews   43
Interview notes   45

Chapter 4: Lodgers (LIL)   46

Background   46
Did you know? Lodger facts   50
Lodgers – the basics   50
The process of taking in a lodger   55
When your lodger moves out   64
Checklist   66
From one live-in landlord to another   67

Chapter 5: The Language of Flatsharing   72

Administration fee   72
Agent   72
Assured short-hold tenancy   72
Assured tenancy   73
Bedsit   73
Bills included   73
Buddy up   73
Bungalow   73
Buy-to-let   73
Buy-to-share   74
Co-buying   74
Contents insurance   74
Contract   74
Conversion   74
Cottage   75
Council tax   75
Credit check   75
Deposit   75
Detached   75
Double room   76
DSS   76
En-suite   76
Eviction   76
Ex-local authority   76
Fixed term   76
Flat   77
Flatmate   77
Flatshare   77
Fractional letting   77
Garden flat   77
Granny flat   77
HMO   78
House   78
Houseboat   78
House rules   78
Houseshare, house share   78
Inter-sharer agreement   79
Inventory   79
Joint and several   79

Key (or card) meter   79
Landlord's insurance   79
Live-in landlord   80
Live-out landlord   80
Lodger   80
Loft apartment   80
Maisonette   80
Mansion   80
Master bedroom   81
Mews   81
Mon–Fri renting   81
No DSS   81
Party wall   81
PCM   82
Penthouse   82
Periodic tenancy   82
Postcode   82
Purpose built   82
PW   82
References   82
Rent a Room Scheme   83
Re-signing fee   83
Room contents insurance   83
Roommate   83
Room seeker   84
Seasonal lettings   84
Semi or semi-detached   84
Sharers   84
Short-term let   84
Single room   84
Speed Flatmating ®   85
Studio or studio flat   85
Sub-let   85
Tenancy agreement   85
Tenancy Deposit Scheme   85
Tenant   86
Terraced house   86
Townhouse   86
Viewing   86
Walk-up flat   86

Interlude: Fighting Over the Remote –Flatshare on the Box   87
Film   87
TV   88
Opera   91

Chapter 6: Living Together   93
Cleanliness   93
Noise levels   99

Money and bills 100
Space and privacy 100
Conflict 102
House rules 105
Lodgers in your home 105
What to do if you can't resolve the conflict 106
A voice of experience 107

Chapter 7: Finance and Bills   108

Rent 108
Deposits 110
Bills 110
Food and shopping 118
Strategy 118
Getting behind with your bills 119

Chapter 8: Contracts, Rights and Agreements   122

Sharers 122
Lodgers 126
Deposits and Tenancy Deposit Schemes 127
Inventories 129
HMOs 130
Your rights 131
Harassment 134
Problems getting hold of your landlord 137

Chapter 9: Flatshare in London (RS)   138

A few common questions 138
Finding accommodation in London 139
How to look 146
Staying safe 149
New to London 150

Chapter 10: Staying Safe   160

Online safety 160
General security tips 162

Useful Resources and Links   167

Flatshare and related sites 167
Information and advice 167
Useful tools 168
London links 168

Appendix: London Postcodes   169

Index   173

Preface

The death of the largest ad site in the world

It's a cold morning in January 2009 and 'The Largest Ad Site in the World' seems sadly deserted – just one woman, in her 50s, is browsing the few hand written window cards. This is not your ordinary newsagent's window; the massive purpose built glass display (in a passageway to the side of an Earls Court newsagent) is designed to house hundreds of private ads.

When I last came here, five years ago, you couldn't get into the passage due to all the eager room seekers slowly shuffling their way around the displays, notebook in hand, jotting down numbers. I had come (in 2004) in the hope of striking a deal with the owners to display an A3 sized poster for my new website (www.SpareRoom.co.uk) for several months – surely the size and extended period warranted some discount? No – they were too busy to need my business. It wasn't just the flat hunters jostling for space, the ads too were packed tight, often overlapping each other. Today the cards are sparse, with more ads for 'services' than rooms to rent.

In 1997, when I first moved to London, reading window cards was one way of finding a room. It wasn't the easiest or most convenient way to look though. For a start you had to know where you were looking to live, as rooms in shop windows are invariably very local ads, and if you didn't already live there you'd have to do a lot of travelling to keep up with the latest offerings. I hadn't a clue where to live – the only areas I knew by name were the famous central tourist areas, not the obscure suburbs of South-East London that my budget could stretch to.

There was also 'Capital Flatshare' – a list of rooms for rent compiled by Capital Radio that you could pick up each Thursday from their Central London offices (again, not massively convenient).

The main method back then was *Loot*, a classified ads paper, which came out several times each week. It contained hundreds of room adverts; around 30 words per ad with no pictures. It left a lot to the imagination, even if you could decipher all the strange abbreviations people used in order to pack more information into the space. The ads began with the place name or postcode in bold and sorted alphabetically. These unheard of places were unhelpful enough to an outsider, but postcode obsessed Londoners listing just the postcode for their location was a real culture shock. To the rest of the country a postcode was just some cryptic code required by the Royal Mail to deliver your post more efficiently, not how you described where you lived.

So, working through *Loot* ads required both an A–Z and tube map to cross reference with and, by the time you'd narrowed down your list and picked up the phone, more often than not the room or flat would've gone already. This is the real limitation of print advertising for flatshares (especially in a busy market like London) – it's out of date before it even goes to press.

I had recently been introduced to the Internet (it *was* 1997) and had immediately become very excited about the possibilities. The way it could improve the process of looking for somewhere to live was obvious: photos; unlimited wording; interactive maps; clever searching and filtering and, of course, bang up-to-date listings. Given the right critical mass, it would greatly reduce the fuss and frustration involved – so, www.IntoLondon.com (the first London flatshare website and, quite possibly, the first flatshare website full stop) was born.

This was the late 1990s, a time when the media was still speculating whether the Internet would just be another CB radio (all set to revolutionize the way we communicate but, in the end, only used by a handful of enthusiasts), so critical mass was some time off. Popularity grew quickly though, as more and more people bought their first computer and dial up connection. Five years later that critical mass was reached and we launched www.SpareRoom.co.uk as a national version of the site.

So, despite the crowds, what I actually witnessed in 2004 at the largest ad site in the world was the death throes of the old age of flat hunting.

The Internet hasn't just revolutionized the way we find a room or flatmate though. The Internet has brought flatsharing out of the shadows (as it has done with so many other areas of life that are slightly left of mainstream), changing its image and broadening its appeal. What was once a rather apologetic way of living, seen as the preserve of students and penniless young graduates, has become not only acceptable but also desirable for professionals both young and old. Reasons for (and attitudes towards) sharing have changed and, now, it's as likely to be a lifestyle choice as a financial necessity. Professionals who could afford to live on their own will now often choose to rent a room in a flat or house share either for the company, to help save for a deposit or to get a better standard of property or location for their money.

The landscape of flatsharing is changing in all sorts of ways and for all sorts of reasons. Over the last ten years we've seen the average age of sharers slowly increase, as more of us stay single for longer and divorcees turn to sharing to rebuild their independence and social life. In the last property boom we saw young professionals looking for a lodger in order to skip the first rung of the property ladder and afford to buy a more attractive two-bed property. Now the boom is over we're seeing more reluctant homeowners joining them in order to keep up with mortgage repayments.

The average SpareRoom.co.uk user now is a 32-year-old professional on a good salary, living with other young professionals in a comfortable two or three bedroom flat. That's not to say our users are average – we've helped hundreds of thousands of people find somewhere to live or someone to share it with including: hedge fund managers, white witches, naturists, families, pensioners and single mothers. The rooms we've helped fill include ones in the wing of a stately home, city centre penthouse apartments, houseboats and hostels. One thing is for sure, there's a flatshare out there for everyone.

Rupert Hunt – Founder of www.SpareRoom.co.uk

How to Use this Book

This aim of this book is to provide you with all the information you need to identify, find and live in any type of shared accommodation. Whether you need a room in a shared house, someone to replace a departing flatmate or a lodger for your spare room, all the information you need is here.

As the book caters for several types of reader, with different needs, not all the information will be immediately relevant to everyone so there are three main ways of using this book:

Read it straight through

If you're new to the world of sharing you could do worse than to read the book straight through. This will give you a good idea of the different types of share and a sense of what living in each is like, followed by advice on finding the right place to live and what to do once you're in. Having found out a bit about all the options, you can re-read the chapters you think are particularly relevant to help you find the best accommodation to suit your needs.

Chapters of interest

If you've got a more specific idea of what you're looking for then you'll probably want to read the most pertinent chapters first. To help you do this we'll point out on the contents page which groups it will be most useful to. The following abbreviations will be used:

SH – Chapters particularly suitable for sharers and flatmates.
RS – This indicates content aimed primarily at those looking for a room (often known as room seekers).

LIL – If you're looking for a lodger then chapters marked LIL (short for live-in landlord) will be the place to start.

You shouldn't just read the chapters you think are aimed at you, if you're thinking of becoming a lodger (for example) reading the chapter aimed at those looking to take in a lodger will give you some insight into their thought processes and should ultimately help you understand each other when it comes to living together.

Some chapters are of interest to more than one group and are marked accordingly; anything without a specific marking is general information, which will be of use to everyone.

On one or two occasions (most notably the chapters on finding a flatshare and finding a flatmate) information is relevant to more than one group. If we feel there's a possibility you might miss it (for example you might be looking for a flatshare and skip the chapter on looking for a flatmate) we've kept it in both relevant sections. In most cases we'll mention the topic briefly and point you to the chapter where you'll find the information in full.

Index

At the back of the book you'll find an index so, if there's a particular topic you need information on, you'll be able to navigate to it quickly.

There's also a glossary (Chapter 5, *The Language of Flatsharing*) you can refer to if there are any terms you aren't familiar with.

FLATMATES OR HOUSEMATES?

Rather than stick to one or the other throughout the book, we decided that (as both are commonly used and fairly interchangeable) we'd use whichever seemed to fit in a certain situation or, failing that, whichever sprang to mind first. Technically whichever you use depends on whether you live in a flat or house but usage tends not to be so strict in practice.

FURTHER RESOURCES

At the back of the book you'll find a list of useful resources for handy reference. Most of these will be mentioned in the relevant chapters but we've collected them all together for ease of use. Additionally there are several links to sections of the book (such as checklists) that are also available online. These are mentioned alongside the relevant information as it occurs in the text.

Introduction:
Flatsharing – The Basics

What is flatsharing?

Simply put, flatsharing is a group of (generally unrelated) people joining together to rent a property. If it's a flat it's known as a flatshare and if it's a house (you guessed it) a houseshare – the people you share with are your flatmates or housemates. These terms have all become pretty interchangeable so don't worry about which you use, we generally refer to SpareRoom.co.uk as a flatshare site even though many of the rooms listed are in houses.

Why flatshare?

There are many reasons why people choose to live in a flatshare and most of them fall under the broad categories of funds, flexibility and friendship.

FUNDS

Flatsharing is an affordable way to live (much more so than renting somewhere on your own) so, for many people, it's the perfect option. Whether they're on a budget, paying off student debt, saving for a deposit or just making their money go as far as possible, thousands of people in the UK choose flatsharing as the best option. In recent years, rising house prices have prevented many young professionals from getting on the property ladder so they choose to share. Now house prices are falling many of the same people are either finding it difficult to get a mortgage, waiting to see what happens to the market, or simply finding that sharing suits them at this stage in their lives.

FLEXIBILITY

Sharing with other people gives you so many options for how and where you want to live. You can choose how large a property you live in and how many people you share it with and whether you want a quiet retreat or a vibrant party house. Often you'll find that areas that are way out of your price range on your own become affordable if you share. This is also the case with the type and quality of property you'll find in many cases.

Sharing doesn't usually tie you into long contracts or require you to commit large sums of money so it's the perfect option if you're not sure where you'll be in a year's time. This isn't just the case for younger people, we're seeing more and more older sharers taking advantage of the flexibility offered by sharing, whether they're recently divorced or separated and need somewhere to live while they sort themselves out or needing to move for work but don't want to buy and settle long term in an area. We're also seeing an increasing number of people who rent somewhere near their work whilst keeping a permanent property elsewhere.

This flexibility, and its appeal to all age groups, is evident at the Speed Flatmating events we run in Central London. A recent event spanned all ages from late teens to early 60s and the variety of rooms on offer (in terms of price, location and type of property) had something to suit most (if not all) situations.

FRIENDSHIP

The final F-factor, friendship, is not one to be overlooked lightly. We've spoken to thousands of sharers over the years that choose their lifestyle based of the other Fs (funds and flexibility) but cite friendship as one of the things they've gained most from by sharing. One successful young professional (in her early 30s) we spoke to recently revealed that she was looking for a lodger for her spare room not because she needed the money but because she just wanted someone else around the house.

We constantly hear from sharers who have found some of their best friends through sharing and, by the time you read this, we should have had our first SpareRoom wedding (or the first we know of at any rate).

Who lives in flatshares?

The simple answer to this is 'pretty much anyone'. SpareRoom's two million plus users range in age from school leavers to pensioners and include couples as well as single people. The main body of our users are young professionals (the breakdown on the site at the moment is around 70% professional to 30% student) but flatsharing is popular with all sorts of people looking for somewhere to live.

You'll find ads on SpareRoom from:

- students
- graduates
- young professionals
- immigrant workers
- families renting out a room
- live-in landlords looking for a lodger
- recently divorced or separated people
- retirees
- people relocating for work
- those looking for a room Monday to Friday only
- people visiting the UK from overseas
- couples.

Whatever your situation, there will be a flatshare out there to suit you or the perfect flatmate or lodger. With so many on offer, it can be daunting knowing where to begin looking so we've filled this book with as much advice as we can based on our ten years of running flatshare websites. We hope it will help you in your search whatever you're looking for.

Matt and Rupert

CHAPTER ONE

Types of Let

The term flatshare is widely used in the UK to describe any shared accommodation, not just flats. Similarly the term 'flatmate' is the most commonly used word to describe someone you share with ('room-mate', a commonly used term in the United States, is only generally used in the UK to denote someone you actually share a room with – see below).

Regardless of the terms used to describe them, there are a few basic types of share you'll come across, and each will be discussed in detail in the following pages. Knowing which type of share is the right one for you will be vital when it comes to looking for somewhere to live (see Chapter 2, *Find a Flatshare*) so consider each carefully and how it meets your needs. Different types of tenancy suit different people and have their own characteristics. Certain types of share are more common in some parts of the country than others (although you'll probably find every type of share there is in London – see Chapter 9, *Flatshare in London*).

Flat or house share

This is one of the most common forms of share and is usually the first one which springs to mind when people think of living together. The property is rented out as whole by a group of (two or more) sharers under a joint tenancy. In most cases each sharer has their own room and facilities such as kitchen, bathroom and living room are shared. It's not uncommon for living rooms to be used as extra bedrooms to help keep individuals' rents down as the monthly rent is for the whole property, not by the room. It's also common for sharers to pay different amounts (usually mutually agreed between them) based on the size of their room and any extra benefits such as en-suite bathrooms. This can be a convenient way for groups of friends with different income levels to share a property.

Generally flatshares of this type are great for groups of people who already know each other. Similarly, you'll often find situations where two smaller groups, maybe two pairs of friends, join together to rent a property. This can work well as larger properties are often better value for money than smaller ones. This makes sense if you think about it; two people still need a kitchen, bathroom and living room. A four or five bed house may well have an extra bathroom or toilet but will still generally only have one kitchen and living room so the cost of these 'extra' rooms is split between more people.

Renting by the property rather than the room can have drawbacks. Tenants are often 'jointly and severally liable', which means that anyone (or all tenants) can be held responsible for the rent payments and any other obligations of the contract, such as utility bills or council tax. Things can also get tricky if one flatmate wants to leave before the others, as their notice has the effect of ending the tenancy for everyone and a replacement contract (with a replacement flatmate) is not an automatic right. However, landlords (or their agents) generally allow a replacement flatmate to be found and the contract to be re-signed. See Chapter 8, *Contracts, Rights and Agreements* for more on tenancy agreements.

There is an unwritten code that says a departing flatmate must do all he or she can to find a replacement so as to cause the other flatmates as little inconvenience and expense as possible. As a result you'll see room offered adverts placed by a departing flatmate trying to fill their room before they move out. You'll also find rooms advertised by the existing flatmates as, after all, it is they who will be living with the new flatmate so they'll be keen to be involved with choosing who moves in.

If you're renting a whole property between you the chances are you'll have an 'assured shorthold' tenancy. This is the most common form of tenancy agreement in the UK and the good news is it's covered under the recent Tenancy Deposit Scheme laws (see Chapter 8, *Contracts, Rights and Agreements*). If you're moving into a property to replace a departing tenant it's important to check you're covered by an agreement of some kind as, if the paperwork isn't amended and the old flatmate is still named, you may find yourself in a tricky situation and discover you have no rights.

PROS

✔ Bigger properties are usually better value per room than smaller ones.

✔ You don't have your landlord living with you.

✔ Often the most sociable way to live.

CONS

✗ Lack of privacy.

✗ Sharing facilities with several people.

✗ You may be jointly responsible for rent and bills, which can cause problems if one member of the house falls behind or doesn't pay up.

Rooms for rent (live-in landlord)

Lodging is one of the oldest forms of shared accommodation as we know it and consists of a homeowner living in a property whilst renting out one or more rooms to tenants (known as lodgers). Due to the government's Rent a Room Scheme (see Chapter 7, *Finance and Bills*) allowing owners to earn up to £4,250 per year tax free by taking in a lodger, this arrangement has become extremely popular again. SpareRoom used to get most of its listings from people looking to replace an existing flatmate but now the live-in landlord accounts for over half the 'rooms offered' listings on the site.

In the past it was common for live-in landlords to take in several lodgers and often provide extra services such as laundry and meals. Women often depended on this for an income and, more often than not, lodgers were male.

Today you're just as likely to find a young professional (or couple) renting out the spare room(s) in their flat to help cover the mortgage. In cases like these the living arrangements can be far more like living in a flatshare than the traditional image associated with lodgers. For example, it's not standard practice for meals to be included with your rent today (although some landlords will still offer this service). It's also not uncommon to find older couples or families renting out a room in their family house, perhaps the room of an older child who has left home.

Living with your landlord can be very different from living in a standard flatshare (especially if you're the only lodger) but can be the perfect arrangement for many sharers. If you're living as a lodger in a two-bed flat then it becomes even more important to make sure you find the right person to share with. Similarly, for a landlord, it's vital to choose the right lodger to minimize hassle. It's rare to find a two-bed flatshare made up of strangers (unless one is the landlord) for the very reason that it's an unusual way to live. Add to that the fact that one of you is the landlord and the need for caution is obvious.

A lodger's dodgy experience

'My landlord lived on the top floor and he didn't have a door to his room but had a staircase. My room was at the bottom of the staircase and I could hear his girlfriend telling him "don't be shy!" I was hysterical!'

Amy

Advice for landlords on taking in a lodger can be found in Chapter 4, *Lodgers* and tips on choosing the best lodger can be found in Chapter 3, *Find a Flatmate*.

The landlord's experience

Owen is an actor in his 30s living in South-East London. He bought a flat just under two years ago with the intention of renting out the second room to help with the mortgage. 'Acting is a notoriously insecure career' he says. 'I'd inherited a small amount of money and just been paid for an advert I'd been in. Between the two I managed to get a deposit together which was enough to buy a two-bed rather than a one-bed. By renting out the second room I can cover the difference in mortgage repayments and know I've got some security. I didn't know about the Rent a Room scheme until recently and that's made things much more affordable.'

PROS

✔ Often better quality accommodation as the landlord has to live there too.

✔ Can feel more like a home for the same reason.

✔ If anything goes wrong the landlord is on hand to sort it out.

CONS

✗ Can feel like you're a guest in someone else's house so can be more difficult to invite people back after the pub or have your partner stay over.

✗ If you get on well financial issues can get in the way of your friendship.

✗ Generally sharing with fewer people (often just your landlord) so can be uncomfortable if you don't get on.

Rooms for rent (live-out landlord)

Some landlords prefer to rent their properties by the room. This basically means that each tenant (or couple if they're sharing a room) has an individual contract for their room and all other facilities are shared. The benefit to landlords is that, if one person moves out, it doesn't necessarily mean the whole property will become vacant. Landlords also usually make more renting by the room than renting their property as a whole.

For sharers, there's the bonus of having your own contract and not being responsible for anyone else's rent or share of bills. It also makes for a convenient way for someone on their own to become part of a houseshare without moving in with an already established group and feeling like the odd one out. On the other hand, you may well be sharing with a group of people who don't know each other that well so, if you prefer a social house, it may not be the best option for you.

Traditionally this type of let catered to the lower end of the housing market but, increasingly, landlords are targeting the professional market. Professional landlords and specialist companies have started to offer properties, often new builds, in areas designed to appeal to young professionals. The properties are let by the room and generally furnished to a higher standard than average.

If you're part of a group and are renting rooms in a property without filling it, be aware that the landlord will probably have the right to fill any vacant rooms without telling you first or giving you any say in the matter.

```
┌─────────────────────────────────────────────────────────────┐
│                        Sharer's view                          │
│ 'A few years ago I was sharing a four-bed house with two      │
│ other friends. We each had separate contracts and all was     │
│ fine for six months. Then one day, while I was in the kitchen │
│ washing up, the front door opened and someone came in. He     │
│ said "Hi, I'm Tony, your new housemate". Turns out the agent   │
│ had let the other room and hadn't even warned us so a         │
│ complete stranger just let himself in with his own key and we │
│ had no idea whatsoever.'                                       │
│                                                          Tim  │
└─────────────────────────────────────────────────────────────┘
```

PROS
- ✔ Great if you don't already have people to share with.
- ✔ Means you're not responsible for anyone else's bills or rent if they fail to pay.
- ✔ Often a choice of differently priced rooms within one property so you can work to budget very effectively.

CONS
- ✗ Not always the most sociable way to live.
- ✗ Can have a higher turnover of flatmates, leading to a less settled flatshare.

Bedsits

Bedsit is short for 'bed sitting room' and is exactly that – a room which functions as a bedroom and living space in one. Essentially it's like living in a shared house, rented by the room but you have your own (lockable) room, which will typically have more space than a basic bedroom. Bedsits may have cooking facilities but this can involve nothing more than a microwave and kettle. Most bedsits were created by subdividing larger properties into small, cheap units without too much expense in conversion costs, therefore bedsits tend to be towards the lower end of the housing ladder.

Initially bedsits satisfied a demand created in the years after the Second World War. As people began to feel the need for more personal independence there was a shift away from the traditional boarding house towards more self-contained accommodation, without communal dining and relying on your landlady for meals. This didn't lead to totally isolated living conditions, however, as you'd still be likely to run into your neighbours on a regular basis. In fact the sitcom *Rising Damp* was born out of a situation such as this (see *Interlude: Fighting Over the Remote – Flatshare on the Box* for more on this and other flatshare inspired films and TV shows).

Bedsits have a reputation for being somewhere near the bottom end of the housing market and conjure up images of miserable Smiths fans gazing out of the window at the gasworks, writing poetry and contemplating suicide. The Moody Blues referenced this perception of bedsits in the song *Nights in White Satin*:

> Bedsitter people look back and lament,
> On another day's useless energy spent.

In truth there's a wide range of bedsit accommodation out there and it can provide an affordable option for those on a low budget and new to an area. In many respects bedsits aren't strictly 'shared' accommodation in the same sense as most flatshares, as you won't necessarily have a communal living area, but they are an extension of lets 'by the room'.

PROS
✔ Cheap.
✔ Self-contained up to a point so more privacy than a typical flatshare.

CONS
✗ Can feel isolated.
✗ Not generally the most comfortable places to live.

Room shares

A room share takes things that one step further, meaning you share your bedroom with someone. Generally, this option is taken up by students and overseas visitors staying in London on a tight budget (though, let's face it, most visitors to London are on a fairly tight budget!) and is usually only survived for short periods. Certainly not to be recommended with anyone you don't know extremely well (or aren't prepared to get to know extremely well).

PROS
✔ Generally the cheapest of all the options.

CONS
✗ Sharing a room with someone!

Mon–Fri lets

One trend which has increased in recent years, particularly (although by no means exclusively) in London, is the Monday to Friday let. Basically, this works the same as a standard let but the room is only rented during the week and the tenant is elsewhere at weekends. This can work well for both parties as the landlord (usually a live-in landlord in this case) gets their weekends to themselves and can use the room for visiting friends and family whilst still earning a regular income from it. The lodger gets the flexibility of having somewhere to stay near work during the week at a reduced price and can go home for the weekend. We even heard of one person who lived with his family on the Costa Del Sol and flew back to London on Sunday nights for work on Monday morning. He'd leave a bit early on Friday and be at the beach bar in time for an evening drink!

These lets are often used by people who have a home and family life in one place, but are required by work to spend a lot of time in another location. London is the largest market for this type of let (see Chapter 9, *Flatshare in London*) but anywhere with a large employer (airports, hospitals, universities) can create a demand for this type of room.

```
The landlord's view
'I must admit that it is for financial reasons rather than social and I am out so much during
the week it seems crazy not to earn some pounds on my rather lovely spare room. I tend
to be around more at the weekends and want the flexibility to have family or friends to
stay. It helps towards the mortgage and gives you the flexibility to either have folk to stay
at the weekends or just be on your own – because, let's face it, we don't always feel like
making small talk or closing the bathroom door! It seems that there are a growing number
of people who just work in town during the week and don't want to pay for a full-time rent
so it's a win–win for everyone as far as I can see!'

                                                                              Rachel
```

PROS
✔ Flexible and often cost effective if you need to be in two places.
✔ Can save hours of travelling time.

CONS
✗ Hard to feel settled during the week.
✗ Can put a strain on home life if you're leaving behind a partner and/
  or children during the week.

A few thoughts on sublets

Subletting isn't exactly a type of let, more a let within a let – hence
the name. In basic terms, if two people rent a three-bed property under
a standard assured shorthold tenancy then rent out the third room,
collecting the rent themselves, this is called subletting. This is not
permitted under most standard tenancy agreements. It does, however,
go on and there will be cases where the landlord has agreed (perhaps off
the record) for it to happen. It can also suit people in certain situations
where neither party wants any commitment as there are no contracts
involved. Such a casual arrangement obviously has its risks, the primary
of these being your rights. If you return home one day to find your
flatmates have changed the locks and won't let you back in you won't
have much recourse. On the other hand, without any form of agreement,
your flatmates can do very little about it if you decide not to pay your
rent. In general we'd advise you to steel clear of sublets as they are a grey

and difficult area. If you have three friends with a spare room, you need somewhere to stay and you feel confident the situation is safe then go for it but be wary of sublet arrangements if you're dealing with people you don't know.

CHAPTER TWO
Find a Flatshare

Finding somewhere to live and moving house can be one of the most stressful things you do. Luckily, the finding somewhere part is easier than ever now thanks to the Internet. Rooms in flatshares of all types all across the UK are easy to find, and right now there's a great choice as plenty of people are renting out a room to bring in a bit of extra cash.

Taking a bit of time to work out what it is you're looking for before you start your search will make it much easier to find the right room (and save you a lot of time aimlessly clicking through lists). The basic questions you'll need to answer when looking for a room are 'Where, What and How'. Firstly though you'll need to sort out your budget.

Budget

The factor that will most determine what you look for, and where you look, will be your budget, so it's vital to get this sorted before you do anything else. All this boils down to is working out exactly how much you can afford to spend each month on rent and bills.

Don't forget, some rooms will have bills included in the rent and some won't, make sure you check. If your monthly budget is £400 and you're expecting to pay bills on top of that, then a £450 room with bills included could be a great deal. Without bills included it's simply £50 over budget.

Bear in mind how much you spend every month on travel too. It may well be that you can afford to pay a little more in rent if you're going to be living nearer where you need to be every day and your travel costs will be lower.

Once you've got your budget it'll help narrow down your choices and save some legwork and maybe a little heartache (there's no point viewing and falling in love with a £500 a month room if your maximum budget is £375). It's worth viewing a few slightly above budget, as the perfect place may be worth a little financial hardship (and you can sometimes haggle the rent down a bit) but, in general, stick to searching for places you can afford.

If you need help working out your budget try using an online budget calculator such as the one at: http:/yourmoney.moneyadviceservice.org.uk/tools/budget_planner.html.

Got your budget sorted? Right, here's what's next . . .

What to look for

The first thing you need to decide is what type of property you want to live in. Would you prefer a busy shared house with four or five flatmates or maybe a smaller flat with just one or two other people? Have you considered living as a lodger? Chapter 1, *Types of Let*, will give you all the information you need on the different types of shared accommodation so you should read that to get an idea of your options. In busy areas like London you'll have the choice of all types, but some smaller towns or quieter areas might give you fewer options.

WHAT TYPE OF PROPERTY ARE YOU LOOKING FOR?

What are you looking for? The type and size of property will make a difference to what you can afford and where you can live. As with areas, it's worth thinking about these things first so you can really target your search to find the best place.

Does it matter to you whether you live in a house or a flat? Do you mind living in a tower block and having to use lifts? Often the type of property isn't as important as the features it has so look through this list first and decide which are important to you.

Features

Number of floors

This may seem like a strange one but lots of people don't like sleeping on the ground floor of a building. A house will generally have more than one floor (unless it's a bungalow of course) but flats often have all the rooms on one level.

Outside space

Do you need a garden, balcony or roof terrace? Outside space is great in the summer and is really useful for hanging out washing. In areas with lots of flats and converted houses there will always be more flats without gardens than with (as there's only one ground floor to a building) so you might find something better or cheaper if a garden isn't essential. Often flats will have a communal garden you can use, otherwise is there a park nearby you can use instead?

Parking/bike storage

If you drive you'll need somewhere to park your car. Do you need somewhere off street to park or will you be happy parking wherever you can nearby? In the case of a house converted into flats there are usually more people than parking spaces so always check who gets to use the ones there are, don't just presume that because there is one you'll be able to use it. If you ride a bike you'll need somewhere to keep it that's safe.

Washing machine

Unless you want to cart your laundry to a launderette every week you'll definitely want a washing machine.

Broadband/wi-fi

Most people want Internet access these days and having wi-fi means you can check your emails on your laptop from your own room, which is always a bonus.

Bathrooms

If you want your own en-suite then it will narrow down the number of rooms available to you and will probably cost a bit more as well. On the upside, you won't need to queue to use the toilet or bath so it may well be worth finding an en-suite if you can. This may be something that falls into the 'preferable but not essential' category.

Own front door

If you live in a converted house you may well have one communal front door leading to an internal hallway with individual entrances. This could mean everyone's post comes through the main door and you all have to sort through it to find your own.

These are some of the more obvious points that will help you refine your search, for a list of points to bear in mind whilst actually looking round a specific property see our checklist below.

Size

The other important factor to consider is how large a property you want to live in. Basically this means 'how many people do you want to share with'. If you want a fairly quiet place to live you might want to share a smaller two or three-bed flat. This can put a bit more pressure on the relationship, if you live with just one other person and there's a conflict, there's nobody else to help mediate.

If you like a lot of people around then you'll probably want to live in a bigger, shared house. Larger properties are often cheaper per person than smaller ones but bear in mind you'll have more of a battle to use the bathroom or kitchen if there are several of you.

If you're not too concerned with this point then just search by budget and area and see what comes up.

WHERE DO YOU WANT TO LIVE?

We asked users of SpareRoom what the most important factor in choosing a room was. Fifty-seven per cent said location, twice as many as those who said cost (in second place with 25%).

'I live in a houseshare with four other people. You're probably thinking it sounds noisy, a little bit hectic and that personal space is but a dream. However, the house is large enough to take us, our creative pursuits and our crazy adventures.

With the right mix of people, and a big enough house to accommodate you, the advantages of a large house share far outweigh the negatives. Rent and utilities are more manageable and I have found that you can get better value for your money without compromising personal space. Financial savings are not the only benefits; this style of community living also affords you a friendship network rich in support and fun.

The day-to-day boring bits of managing a large house share can be a potential source of conflict and you're right to presume that there will be times when some housemates feel taken advantage of. In my house we try to avoid this bubbling cauldron of resentment through a cleaning rota and a house kitty that we all share responsibility for. If we have any big decisions to make, we usually cook a house meal, pour a glass of wine (optional), have a natter and then reach a majority decision. From time to time there is the usual flare of temper when somebody hasn't done their weekly clean, a few sarcastic comments about the toilet roll fairy and milk fairy (which I sometimes think are one being), and then there's always the moment when the boredom of compromise sets in – but all in all, this is the general wear and tear of family life and most of the time things run smoothly.

I would best describe my house share as like *Friends* but without the affairs and television cameras, because when it works, it really works. However, if you have a housemate that doesn't quite work with the mix, or, the house isn't big enough to accommodate your individual and group space, then the house can become a challenge.

My housemates and myself have reached that fashionable age of thirty-something, and yes you're right, the birthday parties were great; a big house does equal a big party. I only mention age to indicate that a large house share is not the exclusive property of the twenty-something. Perhaps your measure should be, that as long as you are happy to be part of a community and don't mind sharing the responsibility of a large house share, then I would say dust off that welcome mat and let the fun begin.'

Louise

Where you live will be decided by many factors including:

Budget
No matter how much you love a particular area there's no point looking there if prices are too expensive. You may as well be realistic with your budget from the outset as it's unlikely to change just to suit you.

'A couple of years ago I lived in a small, two-bedroom, ex-housing association flat in North London with a friend. When I say small, I mean very small. Space was limited; he left his bike in the lounge for about eight months once because there was nowhere else to put it. On the upside, bills were cheap and there was never a queue for the bathroom. He would spend most nights at his girlfriend's place so I had the flat to myself, which was difficult at first.

Gradually I came to enjoy the extra space. I taught myself to cook, I could watch what I fancied on TV and have friends to stay whenever I liked. When he was around it was great too, I had a great year, we didn't see much of each other but then again we didn't get in each other's way either.'

John

Work/study
Where do you need to be every day? It makes sense either to look close by or within easy reach of direct transport links as the less time and money you need to spend commuting the better.

Friends/family
Do you want to be near people you spend time with? If so do they live in areas you can afford and like?

Facilities
If you need to be able to get to a gym regularly check if there's one in the area you want to live in. Similarly, look for local shops, bars, restaurants etc, especially if you want to be able to go out locally.

Transport
If you need to use public transport then check what the options are. Is there a good bus service or a tube/train station nearby that goes to where you need to be on a regular basis?

Security
Will you feel safe walking home at night? Will your car be safe on the streets? How safe will you feel in the property?

Working out the areas you want to live in before you start looking will help define your search and save time in the long run. If you're really not sure you can always start with a fairly wide search area and see which specific areas seem to fit your needs and budget. It would be worth spending a day or two looking round these areas, if you have the time, to see how you feel about them. Take a friend and look round the local shops, see what the transport is like and have a drink in the local pub. This won't always steer you towards one area but it may well help you discount one or two.

If you're moving to a completely new town or city you know nothing about then try a little bit of Googling to see what you come up with (I

A note on postcodes

In your search for somewhere to live (wherever in the UK you are) you'll find yourself dealing with postcodes as a means of describing where a property is. If you're new to the UK, or don't fully understand the system, here's what you need to know.

UK postcodes have two parts, the first half includes information on the post town and location within it, and the second contains more detailed information of the street and specific location of the property. The first half is the bit that tells you most of what you'll need to know when flat hunting.

The first letter (or two letters) tells you which town the property is in the region of, and the number usually denotes how far from the town centre it is. For example, PR is the code for Preston, Lancashire. PR1 is the first half of the postcode for the city centre, whereas PR6 covers an area of villages a few miles away.

For a fuller description of how postcodes work and (more usefully) a list of what the prefixes mean go to: www.listmasters.co.uk/postcodes.php.

Googled the area I live in as a test and was rewarded with three different local forums, some information on local schools, several articles on local property, and a fascinating Wikipedia entry which I spent half an hour engrossed in when I should have been writing this – Matt).

WHO DO YOU WANT TO LIVE WITH?

Note – Some of this information is repeated in Chapter 3, Find a Flatmate, in a slightly modified form – aimed at those looking for a flatmate but not a room.

It's also worth thinking about who you want to live with. It can often be easier to share with strangers than friends but it really depends on you and what works best. We asked users of SpareRoom who they thought made the best flatmate – existing friends came in at 28%, with someone you don't already know well ahead at 55%.

There are no hard and fast rules so consider all the options.

Points to bear in mind are:

Age range
Do you mind sharing with people much older or younger than you?

Couples
Would you be prepared to share with a couple? Couples can affect the overall dynamic of a shared house (especially if they have a tendency to argue – see below).

Gender
Some people prefer to live in a single-sex household and some prefer a mix. This one is entirely about what works for you, although in larger flatshares it can be a bit much if you have only male or female flatmates.

Occupation
Does it matter to you whether you live with professionals, students or a mixture of both? Bear in mind a mix can affect your council tax bill (see Chapter 7, *Finance and Bills* for more on this).

Pets
Do you want to share with just people or are their animals okay too?

Smokers
Would living with smokers bother you? How about smokers who only smoke outside? (SpareRoom's research has shown that we're becoming increasingly less tolerant when it comes to living with smokers).

Landlords
Living as a lodger, whilst in many ways no different from living as a flatmate, can have a slightly different dynamic due to the fact you're living with your landlord. See Chapter 1, *Types of Let* for more on what to expect from living as a lodger.

Beware the couple

'I don't generally have a problem living with couples but, when one half of the pairing is perfectly normal and the other half is a complete nightmare it can get tricky.

The couple I lived with recently personified the "opposites attract" cliché. He was laid back and fun, whilst she was anal and completely insecure.

She also had a real problem with laundry – just touching a freshly ironed, perfectly folded pile of sheets would provoke a guaranteed screaming hissy fit, a slamming door and half an hour's manic driving around the streets. As for taking her dry washing off the radiators so you could use them . . .

On another occasion he was home late and she was getting progressively wound up. When he finally rocked up at the insanely late hour of 11.45, I was already in bed. I heard him creeping up the stairs but I was nearly deafened by her cry of "Will you be quiet, you're waking up the whole house!"

So, my advice is that living with a couple is risky. Simply put – any housemate carries a certain possibility of disaster but a couple comes as a unit so the odds immediately go up. Tread carefully.'

Sally

THE PERFECT FLATMATE
Choosing the perfect room is the easy bit, choosing the perfect people to share with can be less straightforward, especially if you only have a few minutes during a viewing to get to know people.

There are a few key points to consider, however, to get you moving in the right direction and discount a few obvious mismatches.

Decide what you want from a flatmate

For example, if you are new to the area, you may be flatsharing as a way to create a new social circle and will be looking for someone who shares similar interests and is open to going on the odd night out. On the other hand, you may already have a wide circle of friends in the area and just want somewhere to rest your head, so the age and interests of your flatmate are irrelevant. It's generally best not to expect your flatmates to become your new best friends, if it happens great but don't try and force the issue.

Work out whether your lifestyles will be compatible

If you have to be up early in the morning for work and like to go to bed at 10pm, you won't enjoy living with someone who works late and gets home around 1pm with half the local pub in tow . . . and vice versa!

Be honest about how houseproud you're likely to be

You'll get a sense of how clean the existing housemates are from the viewing (although bear in mind, they've – hopefully – tidied up a bit before showing you round). Be honest with yourself, if you view an absolutely spotless flat and you're a bit of a slob then chances are you'll have problems somewhere down the line.

Make sure you meet all of the flatmates before agreeing to move in

Even if you've met two out of three and get on really well with them, you could still find you hate the third person once you're in and it's too late.

Find out about any house rules and regulations

Be honest with yourself about whether you will be able to stick to house rules. In the interests of harmony, most households will have at least some written or unwritten rules and expectations; however, there will be households where the list is extensive. If you don't like any of the rules on the list, or are unsure you can stick to them all, it's probably better that you don't move in, for your own sake as well as the rest of the household.

Finally, don't move in with someone you are sexually attracted to

If you are attracted to a potential flatmate invite them out for a drink instead; if it doesn't work out at least you won't be stuck living with them.

A cautionary tale

'Be wary of moving into a house purely because the housemate is beautiful. I did and ended up with great sex for two weeks, but, when that cooled off, it was unbearable living in the house. DO NOT sleep with flatmates!'

Benji

HousemateHeaven.com has a fun tool for working out what type of housemate you are and who you'll be compatible with, see: http://www.housemateheaven.com/lifestyles.php.

WHAT AM I LOOKING FOR?

We've prepared a short questionnaire for you to fill in to help you narrow down your search and work out what's most important to you. You can fill this one out, photocopy it so you can use it more than once or print and edit a copy from: www.SpareRoom.co.uk/essentialguide/checklists.

	Definitely not	Don't mind	Preferable	Essential
Budget £				
Preferred areas				
Property has/is . . .				
Outside space				
Parking/bike storage				
Washing machine				
En-suite				
Own front door				
Bills included				
Near a bus stop				
Near a tube/train station				
Wi-fi				
Happy to share with . . .				
Couples				
Pets				
Students				
Landlord				
Single sex				
Mixed household				
Smokers				

Where to look

Now you've got a clearer picture of the type of flatshare you're looking for you'll need to start looking for it.

LOCAL RESOURCES vs ONLINE

Local papers, notice boards and shop windows can be a good way of finding accommodation but it'll be a bit hit and miss regarding quantity and quality of rooms on offer. By far the easiest way to search is online using one of the many dedicated flatshare sites. Not only will you be able to see photos and even video of the rooms on offer, the selection online is greater and updated several times a day so you can be sure you're seeing rooms that are actually available.

If you're moving to a totally new area you'll be able to start your search from a distance using the Internet and do your homework before you get there. This also means you can line up several viewings in a day or two so you can make the most of the time you have if you can only get to the new area for a short time before you move.

Online flatshare listings will also have maps showing exactly where the properties are and have access to a lot more info than you can fit in a print advert or a card in a shop window. It's preferable to use a specialist flatshare site as opposed to a general listings site for several reasons, the most important of these is security.

WHY DEDICATED FLATSHARE SITES?

With so many general classified listings sites around why should you bother with a dedicated flatshare site? General classifieds sites (like Gumtree) are appealing as they can be used without having to register and are a simple way of reaching a lot of people. The downside is that your chances of encountering a scam advert or a fraudulent advertiser are far higher than if you use a reputable site which checks all ads for any scam attempts. At SpareRoom we also require users to register in order to contact you so we have a record of who everyone is. This means that, if a listing does turn out to be fraudulent, we can notify anyone who has been in contact with the advertiser and warn them.

For more information on staying safe using the Internet to find a flatshare, see Chapter 10, *Staying Safe*.

How to look

The best way to search is online and, now you've decided what you're looking for, you'll be able to search far more effectively. If you go to www.SpareRoom.co.uk you'll see a search box on the left hand side of the home page. This will let you search by town or postcode. Try clicking on 'advanced search' as this will give you the option to specify other criteria (such as budget) which will give you better results, especially in areas with a lot of rooms advertised.

If you're in London and need to live near a particular tube line you can search using the Tube Line Tool, which will only show rooms near stations on the line you need. For more on looking in London, see Chapter 9.

By creating a profile on the site you can also sign up for free email alerts, letting you know about any new rooms advertised in your area. This helps you keep on top of your search by having the effect of looking for you while you're busy doing something else.

PLACE A 'WANTED' AD

To make sure you cover all bases you should consider placing a 'room wanted' ad; this will allow people who need to fill a room to find you on the site. Most landlords don't just advertise their room and wait for the emails to flood in, they also search the wanted ads to see who's looking in their area. Placing a wanted ad will also get your details emailed out in alerts to anyone advertising a room in your area and, as most contact on the site comes through room wanted ads, you'll increase your chances of finding the room you're looking for.

Make your ad personal by including some information about yourself so prospective flatmates get some sense of what you're like. Adding a photo to your ad will make people much more likely to click on it – you can even add a short video of yourself.

By giving prospective flatmates a chance to find out a bit about you you'll be more likely to attract the right people. Take these as examples:

Double room wanted
Double room needed in Clapham, near tube. Budget is £500pcm – no smokers.

Outgoing guy looking for a room in a friendly, fun flatshare
Hi, I'm Adam and I need a room (preferably a double) in the Clapham area as I'm moving there to be nearer to work (which is graphic design for the web). I'm hoping to share with a friendly, relaxed bunch who aren't averse to the odd glass of wine, trip to the pub or summer BBQ.

My budget's around £500 a month but a bit more might be possible for the right room with the right people. If you've got a room and think we might get on then get in touch. I'd prefer not to live in a smoking house but smoking outside is fine.
Cheers!

Which gives you a better sense of what Adam might be like as a flatmate? Would you even click on the first one?

BUDDY UP

It's also possible to 'buddy up' online and find other room seekers to share with. Maybe you've found a great three-bed flat that you really want to live in but have nobody to share with – by Buddying Up you can find other people in your situation who'd like to share and form a flatshare of your own. This can also be great if you're a little intimidated by the idea of moving into an existing share where everyone knows each other already. Look out for the blue 'buddy up' links on SpareRoom ads.

SPEED FLATMATING

If you live in London then Speed Flatmating is a great way to meet potential flatmates. It gives you the chance to meet several people in one go in a relaxed and informal setting plus places the importance on the people rather than the property, which can often help you decide which room to go for.

For more information, see Chapter 9.

Professional house shares

A new type of rental accommodation is starting to appear in some of the larger UK cities. These consist of clean modern (often new build) properties managed to a high standard by a professional landlord and regularly include benefits such as a cleaner and Sky TV as part of the package. They're generally only let to professionals and managed to a high standard. Alistair Lawes runs Rooms in Birmingham:

'I choose to rent my four-bedroom houses as multi-let house shares for up to four single professionals. My room rates are fixed and rent includes all bills, maintenance and cleaning; tenants can easily manage their budget and relax in the knowledge that I take care of everything, so it's hassle free for them. This allows me to take control of the bills to make sure they are paid, keep the houses properly maintained and managed and provide the highest standard of cleaning for my tenants – which they obviously appreciate. They enjoy Sky TV with all channels (including Movies and Sports), ultra-high speed wireless Internet, modern appliances and furnishings. The houses are cleaned weekly with carpet cleaning, gardening and window cleaning also taken care of.

My rooms are aimed squarely at single professionals in full-time employment. Single professionals in part-time employment, couples, families including children and those with pets are not accepted. I interview all prospective tenants personally to gauge their suitability as a future tenant of mine.

This way of renting gives tenants the flexibility to move with their career and change direction quickly if job redundancy or relocation occurs. Being able to budget their accommodation costs for up to six months in advance allows them to plan ahead to stay financially afloat. Living in one of my house shares is a fun and sociable way to meet new people, make new friends and relax in a secure environment.'

Alistair Lawes

For more information go to: http://www.roomsinbirmingham.co.uk.

Similar services are run in other cities, e.g. Manchester: http://www.shareshack.net.

SPAREROOM iPHONE APP

SpareRoom.co.uk has a free iPhone app that makes it easy to find a flatshare on your phone. You can browse room offered ads, contact other users and manage your account, all from within the app. For more details go to: http://london.spareroom.co.uk/iphone-app.

Viewings

Now you've found a few rooms to go and see, it's time to think about viewings. It's important to make sure you ask all your questions while you're there rather than sitting on the bus home thinking 'does the rent include bills – I forgot to ask!'

The first things you'll need to know will most likely be covered by the advert you replied to so, before you arrive, you should hopefully know:

- How much the rent is.
- Exactly where the property is.
- How many other people live there.
- If a deposit is required.

If possible you should make sure all the other flatmates will be there when you go to look round as the people you'll live with will make as much difference (if not more) as the room itself. If there are five rooms but you only meet two housemates when you go to view, then you might not get a chance to meet the others 'til you move in, by which time it's too late if there's a problem of any kind.

ASKING THE RIGHT QUESTIONS

The viewing is the ideal time to ask all the questions you have. Some of these (is there a double bed or a single, is there a washing machine) will be obvious from looking round the property, others you'll have to ask.

Here's a list of things you might need to know. It's far from exhaustive and not all of these will apply to you so pick the ones you think you need and add any of your own to the list:

Are bills included in the rent?

If so, which ones? Will you have to pay for council tax, water rates, electricity, gas, phone, broadband? 'Bills included' is fine but very non-specific.

Will I have to pay a deposit?

Most landlords will ask for a deposit along with a month's rent in advance. The typical deposit is a month's rent but it can go up to six weeks (or occasionally higher) so make sure you know. For more information on deposits, see Chapter 8.

Are there any other costs?

It's not unusual for agents to charge admin fees and costs for checking references. Generally, you'll be dealing with an agent in this case rather than the existing flatmates, so they will have all the details. It's worth asking this question anyway, whoever you're dealing with, just so you can be certain.

Will I need to sign a contract?

Whether you're renting from an agent, a landlord, a flatmate or a friend, it's generally a good idea to have a written contract of some kind. Agents and landlords will generally always expect you to sign a contract but it's not always the case if you're going to be living as a lodger. Contracts aren't just there to protect the landlord, they also secure your rights so, if you're not asked to sign anything, don't immediately think 'great!'. See Chapter 8 for information on the kinds of contract you'll be faced with and what they're for.

Is the furniture that's in the room staying or does it belong to the current flatmate?

This may seem unnecessary but you really don't want to find out you don't have a bed on the day you move in. Most rooms will be offered furnished but you need to know if not.

Is any contents insurance included?

You'll need to make sure your possessions are protected so find out if that's something you'll need to sort out or if there's already insurance for the flat as a whole.

Is there a parking space or somewhere safe to put my bike?

Some residential streets operate residents' parking permit schemes so, even if there's space on the street, you may have to pay and/or apply for a permit. If this is the case there will be signs on the street so have a quick look when you're on your way in or out.

Is there a washing machine?

This should be fairly obvious from your viewing but, if you can't see one, don't just presume there is one.

How often and when is the rent due?

If you get paid monthly then it'll be easier for you to pay your rent monthly. It'll also help to be able to pay soon after your wages come through so you can budget for the month.

Does the flat have access to the garden?

Just because there is a garden doesn't mean your flat has the right to use it. The garden may be communal or solely for the use of the ground floor flat so it's best to ask if outside space is high on your list.

Are there any existing house rules I need to know about?

Some houses have rules and some don't but it's probably a good idea to ask although, generally, the existing flatmates will let you know in advance if there are rules you'll be expected to follow.

Is it okay if my other half stays over occasionally?

If your boyfriend or girlfriend tends to stay with you on a regular basis you should check if this is okay as sharing with one person who turns out to be two can be a problem for some people. In most instances it won't be a problem but there may be an agreement between the flatmates that limits the number of times a week people can stay, so ask.

You can print this list (or copy it so you can edit your own version) at: www.SpareRoom.co.uk/essentialguide/checklists, along with a 'viewing notes' sheet you can print out to keep track of what you've seen – this can be especially useful if you're seeing several properties in one day.

Setting up your own flatshare

You may find, once you start looking for somewhere to live, that you come across friends, colleagues or friends of friends who are also looking for somewhere to live. Maybe you've Buddied Up through SpareRoom or a Speed Flatmating event. If this is the case, and you now have a group of people, it might be easier to set up your own flatshare than try and find one with several rooms available.

All this really amounts to is finding a suitable property and coming to an agreement between you about how you'll divide the rent. All the advice you'll find in Chapter 6, *Living Together* is still relevant as is the information in other chapters such as Chapter 8, *Contracts, Rights and Agreements* and Chapter 7, *Finance and Bills*.

FINDING THE PROPERTY

If you're looking for a whole property then you can still search SpareRoom.co.uk as there are whole flats and houses available. It would make more sense, however, to search: www.FindaFlat.com as this site specializes in whole properties rather than rooms.

You should also check your local estate agents to see which ones also deal with lettings. You'll be able to register your details with them in the same way you would if you were looking to buy, they'll then let you know what they have that would be suitable and arrange viewings for you.

You should be aware that lettings agents, although paid by the landlord not the tenants, will usually charge additional fees to cover certain admin costs (such as checking references).

CHAPTER THREE
Find a Flatmate

Where you live is one of the most important everyday factors that affect your happiness (along with things like relationships and work) and, if there's a problem, it can be hard to focus on anything else. If you live somewhere you don't want to go back to after you've finished work (or don't feel you can relax in), then your chances of being content in your day-to-day life are fairly slim.

Finding the right property can be difficult enough in itself but it's finding the right people to share with that's the real trick to successful flatshares. An okay property with great flatmates can make for the perfect flatshare, but if you live with people you either don't like or get on with, no amount of lovely hardwood flooring and posh kitchen appliances can make up for it.

Sometimes it can be difficult to share a space with people you're really close to, let alone with strangers, so, how do you go about finding a new flatmate? Looking in the right place is a good start but how you look and what you look for are just as important.

Who do you want to live with?

Note – Part of this advice also appears in Chapter 2, Find a Flatshare, in a slightly different form, aimed at those looking for a place as well as people to share with.

FRIENDS AND COLLEAGUES
There are several choices available to you when it comes to finding a flatmate. The first, and most obvious, is to look amongst people you already know. Do you have a friend who needs somewhere to live or a

work colleague perhaps? It's worth bearing in mind that sometimes you can have too much of a good thing, it can be easier to live with people you don't spend all your time with!

Matt says:

'The first flat I shared in London was with my three best friends. We were all in a band together and rehearsed, recorded and stored all our gear in the flat (which had no living room). By the end of the year we were pretty much all ready to kill each other. Luckily we didn't and, once we'd moved into different flatshares, life became much easier! We're all great friends and three of us are still in a band together (the other guy lives abroad now – not because of us I hasten to add). In hindsight we just spent too much time together!'

FRIENDS OF FRIENDS

You may not have any friends looking for somewhere to live (or any friends you want to live with) but your friends and colleagues may well know someone who needs a room. Sometimes the extra distance of knowing someone without being in each other's pockets makes it easier to live together.

STRANGERS

The word strangers makes this option sound far harsher than it is; sometimes people you don't know make the best flatmates. We asked SpareRoom users and 55% said that someone you didn't already know would make the best flatmate (with existing friends scoring 28% of the vote).

Points to bear in mind are:

Age range

Do you mind sharing with people much older or younger than you?

Couples

Would you be prepared to share with a couple? Couples can affect the overall dynamic of a shared house (especially if they have a tendency to argue – see page 37).

Gender
Some people prefer to live in a single-sex household and some prefer a mix. This one is entirely about what works for you, although in larger flatshares it can be a bit much if you have only male or female flatmates.

Occupation
Does it matter to you whether you live with professionals, students or a mixture of both? Bear in mind a mix can affect your council tax bill (see Chapter 7, *Finance and Bills* for more on this).

Pets
Do you want to share with just people or are their animals okay too?

Smokers
Would living with smokers bother you? How about smokers who only smoke outside? (SpareRoom's research has shown that we're becoming increasingly less tolerant when it comes to living with smokers).

THE PERFECT FLATMATE
Choosing the perfect room is the easy bit, choosing the perfect people to share with can be less straightforward, especially if you only have a few minutes during a viewing to get to know people.

There are a few key points to consider, however, to get you moving in the right direction and discount a few obvious mismatches.

Decide what you want from a flatmate
For example, you may be looking for someone who shares similar interests and is open to going on the odd night out. On the other hand, you may already have a wide circle of friends and just want someone to fill the room, so the age and interests of your flatmate are irrelevant. It's generally best not to expect your flatmates to become your new best friends, if it happens great but don't try and force the issue.

Work out whether your lifestyles will be compatible

If you have to be up early in the morning for work and like to go to bed at 10pm, you won't enjoy living with someone who works late and gets home around 1pm with half the local pub in tow . . . and vice versa!

How houseproud are you?

Be honest with yourself, if you like an absolutely spotless flat you're unlikely to see eye to eye with someone who cleans only when absolutely necessary.

Finally, don't give the room to someone you are sexually attracted to

If you are attracted to a potential flatmate invite them out for a drink instead, if it doesn't all work out at least you won't be stuck living with them.

A cautionary tale

'Be wary of moving into a house purely because the housemate is beautiful. I did and ended up with great sex for two weeks, but, when that cooled off, it was unbearable living in the house. DO NOT sleep with flatmates!'

Benji

A WORD ABOUT LIVING WITH COUPLES

Living with couples can drastically alter the dynamic of a flatshare. If they don't get on then it can be extremely difficult, if they do they're likely to take the same side in any house discussions and outnumber you. Additionally, if you let a double room to a couple then there's one more person needing to use the kitchen and bathroom than there would be if you let to a single person (on the other hand, there's an extra person contributing to bills).

We're certainly not trying to put you off living with couples, just consider how it might be different and affect the house as a whole first.

Beware the couple

'I don't generally have a problem living with couples but, when one half of the pairing is perfectly normal and the other half is a complete nightmare, it can get tricky.

The couple I lived with recently personified the "opposites attract" cliché. He was laid back and fun whilst she was anal and completely insecure.

She also had a real problem with laundry – just touching a freshly ironed, perfectly folded pile of sheets would provoke a guaranteed screaming hissy fit, a slamming door and half an hour's manic driving around the streets. As for taking her dry washing off the radiators so you could use them . . .

On another occasion he was home late and she was getting progressively wound up. When he finally rocked up at the insanely late hour of 11.45 I was already in bed. I heard him creeping up the stairs but I was nearly deafened by her cry of "Will you be quiet, you're waking up the whole house!"

So, my advice is that living with a couple is risky. Simply put – any housemate carries a certain possibility of disaster but a couple comes as a unit so the odds immediately go up. Tread carefully.'

Sally

HousemateHeaven.com has a fun tool for working out what type of housemate you are and who you'll be compatible with, see: http://www.housemateheaven.com/lifestyles.php.

Where to look

LOCAL RESOURCES vs ONLINE
Local papers, notice boards and shop windows can be a good way of advertising your room but it'll be a bit hit and miss regarding the number of people who will see your ad. By far the easiest way to advertise is online using one of the many dedicated flatshare sites.

FLATSHARE WEBSITES
Not so long ago you had to rely on local papers and *Loot* to find somewhere to live. It can be almost impossible to get any real sense of what to expect from an ad that's short, e.g:

Tooting Bec – Dbl rm in 3-bed flat nr tube. GCH, fitted kitchen, share w/ 2 guys in 20s. £450 pcm plus bills.

These days it's much easier as online listings allow you to see photos and video of each property along with detailed information on what the room and facilities are like and maps showing the exact location.

Why dedicated flatshare sites?

With so many general classified listings sites around why should you bother with a dedicated flatshare site? General classifieds sites (like Gumtree) are appealing as they can be used without having to register and are a simple way of reaching a lot of people. The downside is that your chances of encountering a scam advert or a fraudulent advertiser are far higher than if you use a reputable site. At SpareRoom.co.uk, we check all our ads thoroughly for any scam attempts. We also require users to register in order to contact you so we have a record of who everyone is. This means that, if a listing does turn out to be fraudulent, we can notify anyone who has been in contact with the advertiser and warn them.

For more information on staying safe using the Internet to find a flatmate, see Chapter 10, *Staying Safe*.

PLACING AN AD

Advertising your room on one of these sites is easy to do and can reach a huge number of potential flatmates (at the time of writing SpareRoom. co.uk has over a million registered users across the UK and overseas).

It's worth taking a little time to make the most of your advert to help it stand out from the others and attract the right flatmate for you. Here are a few tips to get your ad in shape.

Browse some other ads

This should be first on your list. Try doing a search on SpareRoom.co.uk for other rooms in your town, area or postcode. This will help you with several things:

- Checking prices to make sure you're not over- or under-charging.
- Getting an idea of the quantity and standard of other rooms on offer near you.
- Becoming familiar with how ads are laid out and what information you should put in yours.

It'll also help you when it comes to writing your ad. Have a look at some other listings and see which you'd be interested in if you were looking for a room, you can then use these as a starting point. Think why you liked the look of them (good information on local facilities, lots of good photos of the room and flat, a friendly tone of voice etc.) and incorporate that into your own listing.

Take your time

It's important to remember to **take your time** when you write your listing. It'll be tempting to knock something out in five minutes during a break at work but resist – the more time you spend on your ad, the better it will be. At the moment, there are more people looking for someone to fill an empty room than ever so you'll need to stand out from the others.

Give your ad a catchy title

'Double room' says what you've got but 'Bright double in friendly and spacious garden flat' says so much more. If you're advertising in a busy area your ad may have to compete with hundreds of others, so give room seekers a reason to click on yours first.

Price your room to the best effect

Once you've seen what others are charging you should have a good idea of where your room falls in the price scale. Don't forget you'll need to make it clear whether or not bills are included. If they are it's worth mentioning this in the title (e.g. 'Large double in cosy 2-bed flat – BILLS INC'). Otherwise seekers might just glance at the price and think it's a bit steep, not realizing that it's all inclusive.

Know your local market

If you've got a large employer near you (hospitals, airports and universities all fall into this category but there are plenty of others too) then you're likely to find it easier to fill your room. Have a scout around and see what there is nearby; if it's the kind of area a lot of people commute to you might get more responses by offering the room all week or just Monday to Friday (at a reduced rate). This has the added bonus of giving you most weekends free. Universities are always great as they not only employ hundreds of people but also have a steady (and self-renewing) supply of students. Don't forget, not all students want a party house, often final year or post-graduate students will want to retreat somewhere quiet to work when deadlines loom.

Don't just sell the room . . .

A great room is a good starting point but the property as a whole can be just as important so make the most of it. Include photos of the best rooms and mention anything you think might sway people, for example:

- A garden, roof terrace or balcony.
- Multiple bathrooms (always a bonus in a flatshare!).
- Newly fitted kitchen or bathroom.
- Wireless broadband.
- Big flat screen TVs and cable or satellite packages.
- Great views if you're on the top floor of a tall building.

Mention the area too

If there's anything in the area that you think will help sell your room then mention that too. Some examples of things people look out for when they're moving are:

- Great local bars or pubs.
- Good restaurants or takeaways.
- A handy supermarket or local shops.
- A gym.
- Parks.
- Proximity to public transport.
- Cinema.

The more you can convince someone that where you live is a good place to be, the easier it will be for them to imagine themselves living there. Tell them what you like about living where you are.

You get the idea, as always, a quick browse through some of the ads on SpareRoom will give you a good idea of what's considered desirable.

Have a look at these two listings as examples. Which tells you most about the room and what it would be like living there and which would you click on first?

Double room, E3

Double room available in Bow. Has own shower room and flat has a garden. Near tube and shops. £450 pcm.

Lovely bright en-suite double in quiet Bow garden flat

Recently re-decorated double room with its own en-suite shower room (with power shower and underfloor heating). The flat is in a quiet residential road just 4 mins walk from the tube and handy for a great range of shops and bars. There's a garden for sitting out with a glass of wine in the summer and a parking space out front that we don't use (so it's all yours if you need it).

You'll be sharing with 3 young professionals (ages 25–31) who like to share the occasional bottle of wine and cook dinner together sometimes. Rent is £450 a month and this includes council tax. If this sounds like what you're looking for give us a shout!

The second is clearly more interesting (both the headline and the ad text). A real listing has space for much more information than this (and the general information you fill in will also be displayed as well as a map of where you are), but this should give you an idea how much difference it makes if you spend a little time on your listing.

Preparing the room and making the most of photo and video advertising

If you're taking photos and video to upload to your ad then make a little effort. Treat it like a viewing and tidy up first; photos of a nice clean room (and flat) will look better and the room itself will seem bigger if it's not full of clutter.

A quick video tour of the house or flat will help give people a good sense of the layout and what's available. You don't need to be Steven Spielberg to do this, even a quick video shot on your mobile can be uploaded to give potential flatmates a sense of the space.

How to look

BE PRO-ACTIVE

It's not just a case of placing your ad then waiting for the perfect flatmate to call you. Be pro-active and look for people who need a room in your area. Check the 'room wanted' ads to see who's looking for something near you and contact any who look good. You can also sign up to receive alerts from SpareRoom letting you know of any new room seekers in your neck of the woods; by doing this you might just come across someone who missed your ad on the site or hasn't got round to searching yet.

SPEED FLATMATING

If you live in London then Speed Flatmating is a great way of meeting several potential flatmates in one go. The bonus of this method is that you get to spend a little time with people in a relaxed, social setting so you're far more likely to get a sense of what they're like than you would from a five-minute viewing after work.

Chapter 9 is the place to look for information on Speed Flatmating.

SPAREROOM iPHONE APP

SpareRoom.co.uk has a free iPhone app that makes it easy to find a flatmate on your phone. You can browse room wanted ads, contact other users and manage your account, all from within the app. For more details go to: http://london.spareroom.co.uk/iphone-app.

Viewings and interviews

If you've seen the beginning of *Shallow Grave* (see Interlude: Fighting Over the Remote – *Flatshare on the Box*), you'll know that the flatmate interview can be a strange process for both parties. It's tricky to get a sense of someone from such a short process. However, it's often the only chance you get to assess someone's suitability to live with you so make the most of it.

A FEW THOUGHTS ON VIEWINGS

Firstly, make a bit of an effort when someone's coming round to see the room. I wouldn't suggest resorting to levels of preparation some of the property shows go to (light a fire, make a pot of fresh coffee, have some fresh bread just out of the oven, and so on), but a bit of a tidy up should be the least you do. If there's still someone in the room that's being offered get them to declutter as much as possible so the person thinking of moving in doesn't just see their stuff and not notice the room itself.

Secondly, it may not always be possible but, whenever you can, try and have all the flatmates available when you do viewings. That doesn't mean you all have to open the door together and follow your prospective flatmate round while they take the tour but they'll want to meet everyone they might be living with. On top of this, if you're going to share your flat with someone for the next 12 months, you probably want to check them out, don't you?

Thirdly, try not to rush people. You can look round a three-bed flat in five minutes and that's not necessarily enough time to decide if you want to live there so give people a bit longer if they look like they need it and let them ask any questions they may have about the flat, the rent, the area, whatever.

Obviously some people just won't be right for your flatshare and that will be obvious, so don't spend ages with people you think are wrong but don't just shove them out of the door!

You may get the occasional odd viewer as did one of our users a couple of years ago (luckily we don't hear too may of these):

'When interviewing for a flatmate I had a bloke come to see the flat. Before he even got up the stairs he told me that he had a long journey and could he use the loo (fair enough). Twenty-five minutes later he was still in there, after thirty-five minutes he opened the door, said thank you very much and left. Needless to say I bleached everything!'

Charlie

Additionally . . . see as many people as you can. Don't just accept the first person who shows up and is prepared to take the room; this is someone you'll be sharing with for months (if not years) and you may well end up seeing them more than you see your friends. The more people you see, the better your chances of finding someone great.

If someone comes for a viewing and you think they could be good then you could suggest going for a quick drink before they head off. It'll give you a chance to see each other in a more relaxed setting and get a sense of what spending an evening with them would be like.

If someone comes round to see the room and you really fancy them it's probably a better idea to ask them out than let them move in. If you have expectations of what will happen and they're not interested then it'll make things awkward for both of you (especially when they want to bring someone else back with them!). Even if the best were to happen and you fell in love, would you really want to live with your boyfriend or girlfriend from day one of your relationship? Ask them out to the pub and tell them why you're doing it!

Interview notes

We've prepared a simple viewings sheet for you so you can take notes to help you remember each person. It can be downloaded and printed at: www.SpareRoom.co.uk/essentialguide/viewingnotes.

CHAPTER FOUR

Lodgers

*'I shall never, Master Copperfield', said Mrs. Micawber,
'revert to the period when Mr. Micawber was in difficulties,
without thinking of you. Your conduct has always been of the
most delicate and obliging description. You have never been a
lodger. You have been a friend.'
David Copperfield – Charles Dickens*

Background

RIGSBY & CO – GONE BUT NOT FORGOTTEN

When you hear the word 'lodger' what springs to mind? Rigsby from *Rising Damp*; cheap rooms to let; formidable landladies; an album by David Bowie? Although lodgers seem like an old fashioned concept they've been making a huge comeback in recent years – people advertising a room in their own home now account for over half the ads on SpareRoom (it was only a third a few years ago), so why the big increase?

LODGERS TODAY

There are several reasons why people take in a lodger. In these times of financial difficulty there are plenty of people who need a little extra income as well as plenty more who need somewhere affordable to live but don't necessarily want to live in a big shared house. Taking in a lodger can go a long way to helping with mortgage payments, especially with the government's Rent a Room Scheme allowing you to earn up to £4,250 tax free by renting out a room. Plenty of people bought homes in the past few years when good mortgage deals were easy to come by;

as these homeowners need to re-mortgage they're often finding their payments going up and they simply can't afford them any more.

Taking in a lodger can provide an easy source of additional income and is enabling thousands of people to stay in their homes. It's also a flexible solution as you can take a lodger in for three months, six months, a year or however long you need to (and you can have breaks between lodgers if you want) so you're not committing to a permanent change in your lifestyle. Many people also take in a lodger for company as well as money – see Melanie's story below.

WHO TAKES IN A LODGER?

Traditionally we think of lodgers in terms of an older landlord (as often as not a landlady) who rents out several rooms in their house and provides meals for lodgers. While this group still exists there are plenty of other people taking in lodgers today.

People who take in lodgers can be roughly broken down into three groups:

- families and couples;
- young professionals;
- more traditional landlords and landladies.

Families

Often a family with children (perhaps young children or older children who have left for university) has a spare room in their home and decides to let it out for a little extra income. In these cases the situation is very much like living in a family house rather than a flatshare. Meals are sometimes provided, especially if you're likely to be around when the family eats. This type of lodging can be perfect for students who want to live in a family situation rather than a noisy shared house (especially if they have a lot of course work to get through). This type of lodging can also suit younger people looking for a room in a property with a family feel – especially if it's their first experience of living away from home.

How long have you been taking in lodgers and how many have you had?

We took in our first lodger nine months ago and she's still with us now. She's the only lodger we've had.

What have been the best and worst parts of the experience?

Best: Our lodger joining in our family Christmas; having a babysitter on hand.

Worst: My son calling her 'Mummy'!

How has taking in a lodger benefited you?

It has been a huge financial help and has meant we get to stay in our home during these hard financial times. Also, we have made a friend and our children simply love her, which means we feel comfortable going out for an evening and leaving her in charge.

What advice would you give to anyone thinking of taking in a lodger in terms of preparation?

Always conduct a relaxed interview. People will be on their best behaviour when they come to see you but you need to know the real person. Also, don't assume their personal problems (divorce/recent break up etc) will impinge on your life, give people a chance. Make sure the person fits in with your lifestyle (e.g., if you are a 20 something who likes to party, don't have a 50 year old lodger who wants to go to bed at 9pm!).

Can you explain the process you go through when you advertise for a lodger?

We advertised on SpareRoom, then invited people who responded to our home for a cup of tea and a chat, then talked it over in private before advising of our decision.

What kind of questions do you ask prospective lodgers?

What hours do they keep re their job; will there be a boyfriend/girlfriend visiting; do they smoke; do they mind cats; do they like children; are they prone to coming in late ALL the time; where are they coming from (another house? in which case are references available).

How has it been for you overall?

We have been very lucky with our lodger and she fits in with the family fantastically. I think, at the interview, you usually know if you are comfortable with someone, and that's what it's all about. You need to be able to relax in front of that person – if you don't feel like you could veg out in your pyjamas, watching a bad film in front of them then they aren't right to be living with you!

Alex

Young professionals

This type of lodging generally consists of a young professional (or a couple) who has bought a two- or three-bed flat on their own and wants to rent out their spare room. It's far more likely to feel like a flatshare, even if one of you does own the flat, so don't expect your meals and laundry done for you.

'I had lived by myself for a long time and needed to get a lodger. I am the kind of person that enjoys my own company a lot but, if I spend too much time alone, I am in danger of developing strange, anti-social habits. I think it's important to have people in place to keep you in check.

I have had bad experiences in the past with flat mates so it was crucial for me to select the right one. I would always ask a friend for a second opinion but, generally, I would make sure the person is friendly, relaxed and they don't smell bad! In a short space of time you can only go on what feels right – trust your instinct even if you can't articulate it'.

Melanie

Traditional landlords and landladies

This is what we think of when people mention lodgers. Usually it will consist of an older landlord or couple who rent out several rooms in their home, often to students. You're more likely to get meals included in this type of share but it won't always be the case.

'My wife & I are 68 years old and love having paying guests in the house. My wife is a Scottish Tourist Guide and I started a small charity, which keeps me out of trouble. I feed the guests whenever possible so we all eat our evening meal together. When we decided to have paying guests, I took over the cooking and looking after the house – cooking had been a hobby of mine but doing it regularly is very pleasant therapy. Most of my experiences have been quite delightful. When they are not delightful, it is usually my fault – I have not explained the terms of taking the rooms clearly enough, although they were clear enough to me!'

Mark

Did you know . . . ?

LODGER FACTS

We recently conducted a survey of almost 3,000 people in the UK who take in lodgers – here's what we found:

- 62% of those who have taken in a lodger are female
- The biggest age group taking in lodgers are the over 50s at 30%. The overall age breakdown is:
  - 18-24   7%
  - 25-29   13%
  - 30-34   14%
  - 35-39   12%
  - 40-49   24%
  - 50+   30%
- 56% of live in landlords are educated to degree level or higher
- 43% don't have a written agreement with their lodger
- 64% only started taking in lodgers in the past two years
- 15% have been taking in lodgers for five years or more
- 8% have had more than 10 lodgers
- 41% couldn't afford their mortgage without a lodger
- Just 10% have an existing friend as their only lodger

LODGER EXPERIENCES

- 93% said it had been a positive experience
- 94% said they'd do it again
- 60% said they regarded their lodger as a friend

Lodgers – the basics

If you're thinking of taking in a lodger there are a few things you'll need to consider. Some of it's just plain common sense but there are a few things you might not have thought about so, starting with the basics, here's our guide to taking in a lodger.

WHAT IS A LODGER?

A lodger is someone who rents a room in your home without having exclusive rights to any part of the property. Lodgers can have extra services (such as cleaning, laundry or meals) included by agreement but they're not compulsory.

WHAT'S THE DIFFERENCE BETWEEN A LODGER AND A TENANT?

'Lodger' isn't a legal term – strictly speaking your lodger is a licensee. This means they have the right to live in your home but don't have exclusive access to any of it. Tenants, on the other hand, have more rights than lodgers and you, as a landlord, have more obligations, so it's important you don't take someone in as a tenant when they should really be a lodger. The simple rule is not to have a lock on your lodger's bedroom door. This doesn't mean you can wander in and out of their room at will though (not if you want them to keep living with you and paying rent).

WHO CAN TAKE IN A LODGER?

Most homeowners and local authority tenants can take in a lodger but there are several factors to consider before you go ahead. You will need to inform your mortgage lender or local authority and you'll almost definitely need to alert your insurance provider. If you claim any benefits these will probably be affected if you take in a lodger. If you rent you need to check with your landlord to see if your tenancy allows for sub-letting. Most don't automatically but your landlord may be fine with you having a lodger, especially if it stops you falling behind on the rent. You shouldn't need a new tenancy agreement in this instance, a letter of permission from your landlord will be enough.

WHAT WILL I NEED TO PROVIDE?

In the simplest terms you'll provide a furnished room plus use of communal areas and facilities. Other benefits such as cleaning and meals are up to you.

HOW MUCH CAN I CHARGE?

That all depends on where you live and what your property is like. Have a look on: www.SpareRoom.co.uk at other rooms available in your area to get an idea what the going rate is likely to be. At the time of writing, the national weekly average earned in the UK by taking in a lodger is around £94, this equates to £4,888 a year. In London the average is £135 per week or £7,020 per year.

CAN I EVICT SOMEONE IF IT DOESN'T WORK OUT OR I NEED MY ROOM BACK?

The law recognises that, as a live-in landlord, you're more vulnerable if your relationship with your tenant breaks down. That's why, generally speaking, it's easier to evict a lodger than a tenant (you will need to give 'reasonable notice' if you intend to evict).

We strongly recommend a written agreement between you and your lodger(s) so the conditions are agreed upon in advance. The contract should include the following information at minimum:

- The amount of rent you're charging.
- How long the let is for.
- What notice either of you must give if you want to end the agreement.

If you find you have a dispute with your lodger some councils have a Tenancy Relations Officer you can turn to. They can't tell either of you what to do but can mediate to help resolve a situation. See Chapter 8, *Contracts, Rights and Agreements*, for more on evicting a lodger.

WHAT'S SO GOOD ABOUT TAKING IN A LODGER?

The obvious benefit is money; that's why most people take in a lodger. The other positives can be company (especially if you live on your own) and – crucially – flexibility. The great thing about taking in lodgers is that it's entirely up to you how long you do it for. You can rent out a room for six months then have a break, take a few months off whenever your lodger decides to move on, rent Monday to Friday to give yourself weekends free or just take a lodger for a fixed period to help you through a specific financial low point.

WHAT ARE THE DOWNSIDES?

Inviting someone else into your home is always a bit of a risk. The one thing you will certainly lose is a bit of your privacy although, as one cash strapped SpareRoom user said to us recently, it's better to lose a little privacy than to lose your home. By taking a few simple precautions you can minimise the risks and take much of the anxiety out of the process (more on this later in the chapter).

It doesn't always work straight away, but when it does . . .

> 'In the last year alone I have had some dreadful experiences with renting out my spare room. One guy totally took over my lounge and wouldn't let me watch TV or listen to music as he was watching Top Gear re-runs all the time – he left owing me about £300. Since then I have had better luck, and in the past have met some lovely people through renting out my spare room, some of whom are my closest friends now and one of whom is now my boyfriend! So it's not all bad!'
>
> Helen

HOW CAN I FIND A LODGER, IS IT DIFFICULT?
The advent of online flatshare listings has made finding a lodger easier than ever. With an online listing on sites such as: www.SpareRoom.co.uk you can include photos and a video of your room so prospective lodgers can see what's on offer. You can also check out who's looking for a room in your area.

WILL I BE TAXED ON MY INCOME AND DO I HAVE TO DECLARE IT?
Under the government's Rent a Room Scheme you can earn up to £4,250 tax free by taking in a lodger and, provided you don't earn more than this, you won't need to declare it. There's more info on this later in the chapter.

DO I NEED TO COMPLY WITH THE NEW TENANCY DEPOSIT LAWS?
So far the law only applies to assured shorthold tenancies so you can take a deposit (and we recommend you always do) without having to use the scheme.

WHAT ABOUT GAS SAFETY CHECKS AND FIRE REGULATIONS?
If you rent out a room in your home you must make sure that all gas appliances are maintained in good order and that an annual safety check is carried out by someone who is registered with the Gas Safe Register.

Fire Safety Regulations only apply if the property isn't your main residence and is considered primarily as a source of income. You should fit (and regularly test) smoke alarms as a matter of common sense.

SHOULD I WORRY ABOUT HMO?

HMO (or House in Multiple Occupation) refers to a property that's rented by a group of unrelated people. Most flatshares are HMOs. As a live-in landlord your property will only be classed as an HMO if you take in more than two lodgers. Lodgers that are related to you don't count as they're counted as part of your family (the same is true of any domestic staff that live with you, e.g. a nanny or au pair). If you plan to take in more than two lodgers you should look into HMO regulations and whether you will need a licence. A free introductory guide to HMO regulations is available at http://www.spareroom.co.uk/hmo_licensing_guide. For more information you should speak to your local authority planning office as the rules are implemented differently by different local authorities.

One landlord's experiences

Highs of house sharing from a live-in landlord's perspective:

Extra income. I can't stress this enough! Thanks to the tax break I can earn £350 each month without worrying about tax, which is a huge bonus. It effectively doubled my disposable income after all my outgoings. Without it I wouldn't have been able to get on the property ladder.

Flatmates can bring additional skills to the table that you can get at a knock down rate. In the past three years I've have electricians stay (and repair wiring, run in outside lights, wire in power to the garage); a builder (handy van to do tip runs) and an IT engineer . . . very handy for when the laptop crashes!

Lows

Inevitably the burden of sharing space. No tenant will ever treat the house with as much respect as you (as the owner) do.

Past girlfriends have felt threatened by other girls renting a space in the house.

You'll always feel you're tidying up more than just your own mess. No cleaning rotas ever get stuck to.

Awkward if you've got your mum and dad coming to stay and your drunk flatmate has sex with his latest one night stand one floor above them!

... and the lodgers themselves

The first guy that moved in was a bodybuilder. On arrival at home after work I found him fully oiled up wearing speedos sun bathing on the pavement outside the front of the house – on day 1! Also everything he ever touched seemed to have a fine coating of protein powder on it.

I put up a commuter for six months, who was going through a messy divorce. He seemed the perfect tenant, as he was likely to be away at the weekends with his kids. Best thing was, in the first week of his new job, he met a new girl and shortly after moved in with her. In the next five months I only saw him 10 times, so he stayed at my place for less than one night a week, but was happy to pay full rent! Result.

James

The process of taking in a lodger

Okay, so that's the basics covered – now let's look at the process in a little more detail.

Having decided you want to take in a lodger it's important to do your preparation and make sure you've thought everything through. Whilst you can get rid of a lodger if you find out they (or just having a lodger at all) won't work for you, you can put yourself in a strong position to start with, which should eliminate most of the worry. This section of this chapter guides you through the process of taking in a lodger, including how to prepare, interviews, agreements and what to do when your lodger moves out. There's a handy checklist at the end of the chapter to remind you of the main points and some good advice from people who have been through the process themselves.

PREPARING TO TAKE IN A LODGER

Before you take anyone in you should do your homework and make sure you know what's involved in the whole process. Not only does this give you a chance to reflect and decide whether you're ready to get a lodger, it also means you'll be aware of some of the more important stumbling blocks and therefore better prepared to avoid them.

Check you're allowed to take in a lodger

If you own your home then you should be fine to take in a lodger. You must inform your mortgage lender before you do so, however. If you rent then it all depends on the agreement you have with your landlord. Most will prevent you from sub-letting a room as a matter of course but your landlord may well be fine with you taking in a lodger, especially if it means you're more likely to be able to afford the rent on an ongoing basis. Check your tenancy agreement and speak to your landlord – if he gives you permission make sure you get it in writing. It shouldn't be necessary to sign a new contract, a simple letter of permission will be fine.

Local authority tenants should always check before taking in a lodger. It may well be okay for you to do so but it could affect your benefits, leaving you no better off than without a lodger, so make sure you understand the regulations before you do anything.

Inform your insurance provider

There are two main reasons for doing this: to make sure you're still covered and so you can let your lodger know if they'll need their own insurance. Some insurance companies are fine with you taking in a lodger, as long as you let them know in advance, but, in some cases, it will invalidate your insurance agreement. *Always* check first to avoid any nasty surprises further down the line. You may need to change your contents insurance provider in order to get cover with a lodger.

As landlord (if you own your property) you're required to have buildings insurance (and you should have this anyway) but you're not obliged to insure your lodger's personal possessions. If you're happy to include them in your contents policy then that's one option; however, there are plenty of 'room contents' policies around these days, which your lodger can use to cover his or her belongings so that's probably easiest and it saves you adding and removing names every time you get a new lodger.

Inform your local benefits agency

If you receive any benefits it's almost certain they will be affected by taking in a lodger so find out in advance what the result will be.

Let the council know if you're paying reduced council tax for single occupancy

If you pay reduced council tax then your lodger will affect this and you'll almost certainly be liable for the full amount. You can pass this on to your lodger in the rent of course, or as part of the bills they pay. If your lodger is in full-time education or on a government youth training scheme they may be exempt from council tax liability, so double-check with your local authority. Also, if you rent your room on a Monday to Friday basis, and your lodger has another home where they already pay council tax, then your discount should remain the same. You will need to inform your council tax office and you may be required to provide some documentation as proof (such as your lodger's council tax bill from their other property).

Get the room ready

Make sure you have all the furniture you need and everything is ready for a lodger. Remember, if you're going to use the Rent a Room Scheme to earn tax-free income, you *must* provide a furnished room. The minimum we'd recommend is a bed (double if possible), a wardrobe and chest of drawers, a bedside table and a lamp. Most lodgers will appreciate some desk space if there's room but it's not absolutely essential.

Make sure all your own clutter is cleared away as your lodger won't want to live in a room full of your junk. Do this before you have anyone round for viewings.

Most people today have their own mobile phone so you shouldn't have to worry about a phone socket in the room. If you have broadband (and it will be useful if you do) then wi-fi will mean your lodger can access the internet from their room.

Decide in advance what the terms and conditions will be

It may seem unnecessary at first but will avoid most nasty problems before they occur and give you a clear point of reference if you run into any difficulties. This includes you deciding in advance which bills are included in the rent and what else your lodger will pay for.

In addition to financial terms relating to the agreement you should also think about what other expectations you have. Just because you understand what you expect from a lodger it doesn't necessarily follow that they'll presume the same things you do. The more you discuss things up front the less chance there will be of a misunderstanding. Most of the live-in landlords we've spoken to who have had difficulties with a lodger say a lack of communication initially was part of the problem, so make sure you cover as much as possible. Not only does this create a set of expectations you're both aware of, it also gives you a chance to find out what a prospective lodger is like as they may not react as you'd expect them to when you're having the conversation.

Some points to consider:
House rules
This is a broad subject and can cover all sorts of things from who does the washing up to how you buy necessities such as toilet roll and cleaning products. Lodgers may expect you as the landlord to be responsible for these things, whereas in reality, many live-in landlords expect things to be run more along the lines of a traditional flatshare. It doesn't matter how you agree these things but it's always essential to have a frank conversation before you agree to someone moving in to make sure you're both expecting the same things.

Bills
Will your rent include bills or are you going to charge an extra amount for these? If so which bills are included: council tax, water rates, utilities, TV licence, broadband, satellite TV? Don't forget, the amount you can earn tax free under the Rent a Room Scheme includes whatever you charge for bills (if they're included in the rent).

Insurance
Your lodger's belongings won't automatically be covered by your policy – make sure they know this and tell them they'll need their own room contents cover for their possessions to be insured properly.

Guests

Standard lodger agreements usually include a clause stating that overnight guests aren't allowed without your permission. It's reasonable for your lodger to want their partner to be able to stay over occasionally but, if you're not careful, you may find yourself living with a couple and outnumbered in your own home. Make sure you're clear about the rules before someone moves in. If you're happy for their partner to visit and stay over you may want to limit it to one or two nights per week. One live-in landlord we spoke to recently told us he thinks it's fair for his lodger's girlfriend to stay as many nights a week as he stays at hers. Whatever you decide, don't wait till your lodger has moved in to have this conversation.

Pets

Are you happy for your lodger to have a pet? What if they move in and then get a pet once they're in? Make sure you're clear about this from the start.

Smoking

If you're not happy for your lodger to smoke in the house would it be okay for them to smoke outside?

Get a Lodger Agreement

Signing an agreement in advance, so you're both covered, is not a legal requirement but is nevertheless essential. Despite this 43% of live-in landlords don't have a written agreement with their lodger. A lodger contract doesn't need to be a lengthy or complicated document but should set out the basic terms and conditions, including what either of you will need to do to terminate the agreement. The essentials for any lodger agreement are:

- Both your full names.
- The address of the property.
- How much the rent is and whether it's to be paid weekly or monthly (and on what date).
- What deposit is required or has been taken.
- How long the agreement lasts and what needs to be done in order to terminate it.

You can find links to online agreements at www.spareroom.co.uk/essentialguide/lodger.

Check local rents

You need to know what your room is worth so you can set a fair rent that makes it worth your while without pricing yourself out of the market – there's no point in overpricing your room and struggling to find a lodger. Use: www.SpareRoom.co.uk to search in your area and see what other people are asking for similar rooms.

Get your gas appliances checked by a Gas Safe registered professional

You need to get your gas appliances checked before you take in a lodger (and once a year after that). They must be checked by a Gas Safe registered engineer – you can find one at www.gassaferegister.co.uk.

Advertise your room

Go to: www.SpareRoom.co.uk and place your listing. Don't forget to check the 'room wanted' ads and sign up for alerts so you'll be aware of anyone looking for a room in your area. For advice on placing the best advert see Chapter 3.

Viewings

This is one of the most important steps in the process and one you absolutely shouldn't rush through, however desperate your financial situation is. Take your time with viewings. This gives your potential lodger a chance to ask any questions but also gives you a little more time in their company to see what you think of them. It's important not to just accept the first person who wants and can afford the room – you're not selling a car, you're inviting someone to live in your home. If someone looks round and says 'yes' you can reasonably tell them you've got a few other people coming to see the room and you'll let them know. As you're going to be letting a stranger into your home it's worth taking as much time as you feel you need. Tell them when you'll let them know by (and make sure you follow up on this).

Trust your instincts – if you're not sure about someone you can always wait and advertise your room for a little longer. The extra time it takes to find the right person will be worth it in the long run. Why not ask a friend to sit in on the meeting and ask their opinion when the potential lodger has left – another perspective may well help.

One tip we got from a live-in landlord who uses SpareRoom regularly is to invite anyone you get on with to the local pub for a quick drink after the viewing. It'll give you chance to get to know them a bit in a more relaxed situation and see if you think you're compatible. This is a particularly useful technique if you're renting out a room and there will be just two of you in the property as it becomes even more important to find the right lodger.

Have a look at the advice from live-in landlords at the end of this chapter for some great tips on taking in a lodger from those who've done it before.

Holding deposits

If someone wants to take your room but can't move in immediately, then one option is to ask for a holding deposit. This isn't the same thing as a security deposit (see below), it's simply a sum of money given to you by the lodger in order to keep the room for them. Providing everything goes according to plan and the lodger moves in then the holding deposit can be returned or (more commonly) used towards the security deposit or the first month's rent. If the lodger decides not to move in then you don't have to return a holding deposit (although, if your lodger has to pull out due to unforeseen personal circumstances, you may choose to return the deposit if you think that's reasonable). A holding deposit won't be as much as a security deposit as a rule.

Credit checks

Once you've found a prospective lodger you may want to use a credit checking facility. Not everyone does this with lodgers but there are plenty of services available should you wish to. For links to tenant checking resources, have a look at: www.spareroom.co.uk/essentialguide/lodger.

Security deposits

A security deposit is an amount taken by a landlord as a guarantee against damages or unpaid rent at the end of the term. The standard amount taken is one month's rent (although six weeks is also becoming common). As a live-in landlord you don't need to use a tenancy deposit scheme as it only applies to ASTs (assured shorthold tenancies). Unless you have good reason, the deposit should be fully refunded at the end of the term, so you should make sure it's available whenever your lodger wants to move out (so don't spend it thinking you'll replace it at a later date – it's not your money).

It is also standard practice to take a month's rent up front, so your lodger should pay one month's rent plus a security deposit before you let them move in.

Signing contracts and agreeing terms and conditions

Setting out the details of who is responsible for what in advance is highly advisable to avoid any later problems. You should have prepared for this already, so all that remains is going over the agreement with your lodger, making sure you're both comfortable with the terms, and signing it.

Inventory

At this point your lodger should also sign an inventory. This is a list of all the furniture, fixtures and fittings in the room. The inventory is used when your lodger moves out to establish that everything is as it should be and nothing is damaged before you return the security deposit. For full details of inventories, see Chapter 8.

Getting your lodger to set up a standing order for the rent

This takes the personal element out of collecting the rent, which allows you to avoid having to ask for it every month if your lodger is a little disorganised. Money conversations can be extremely awkward, especially for live-in landlords – this simple step stops that from becoming an issue. It also provides a record of all the money the lodger has paid to you, which will be invaluable in the event of any disputes. You should also buy a rent book and keep a note of every payment made – rent books are available cheaply in shops like WH Smith as well as online.

Lodger moves in

It's a good idea to be available for your lodger on the day they move in – don't just give them a key and go out. They're bound to have questions on the first day so make it easier for them to move in and feel settled –

don't stand around and watch them unpack but make sure they know your door is open if they need you.

Inform your tax office if you earn over £4,250 a year from your lodger

The Rent a Room Scheme allows you to earn up to £4,250 a year by taking in a lodger without paying any tax. If you earn more than this you'll need to declare it.

How does the scheme work?

You let out a room or part of your main property

This can be a whole floor but not a self-contained flat.

It must be furnished

Unfurnished rooms don't qualify under the terms of the scheme.

You don't have to be a homeowner

As long as you have your landlord's consent you can take advantage of the scheme as a tenant. Check your tenancy agreement first or, if in doubt, ask your landlord.

Nothing to declare

If you don't normally fill out a tax return and the income is below £4,250 (around £350 a month) you don't even have to do anything, the exemption is automatic. If the amount you earn is above just let the tax office know.

If you're not PAYE

If you usually fill out a tax return you should consider whether you're better off in the scheme or not. Under the scheme you can't claim expenses for wear and tear, insurance and so on, so you may be better paying tax under the rules for residential lettings. This will enable you to offset certain expenses incurred against income. If you usually fill out a tax return and have an accountant, you should check with them to see whether you'd be better off under the scheme or not.

If you charge your lodger extra for meals or laundry services this all counts towards your £4,250 so bear this in mind. In addition, if you take in a lodger and co-own your property (with your partner, for example) then the allowance is split between the two of you – you can't earn £4,250 each without paying tax.

For full details of the scheme, see: Direct.gov.uk.

Raise the Roof

In 2009 SpareRoom.co.uk (backed by Shelter, The National Landlords' Association and TV presenter Sarah Beeny) set up Raise the Roof, a campaign aimed at lobbying the government to raise the tax threshold of the Rent a Room Scheme. The current amount you can earn tax-free by taking in a lodger (£4,250 a year) was set in 1997 and hasn't been increased since. With rising rents and inflation this means many live-in landlords are either forced to charge below market rate for their rooms or fill out a self-assessment tax return for the small amount above the threshold they make. With recent spending cuts the Treasury decided this was not a priority at the moment but we'll keep bringing the issue up – the longer the amount you can earn tax-free remains static, the less of a benefit it becomes.

When your lodger moves out
WHAT HAPPENS NOW?
Sooner or later you or your lodger will decide it's time for them to leave. In most cases the relationship will end amicably but there are still a few things you'll need to know.

ENDING THE AGREEMENT
Your agreement with your lodger should contain details of what needs to happen in order for either party to terminate the arrangement. Standard procedure is to have a notice period of four weeks – this will give your lodger time to find somewhere else to live. It's possible to insert a clause that gives a shorter period (say two weeks) so either party can end the agreement early if they need to. Otherwise you'll find yourself at the end of the agreed term and you'll need to decide whether your lodger wants to stay (and sign another agreement) or leave. It's worth having a conversation about this before the end of the term so you both know what the other's plans are.

RETURNING THE DEPOSIT

When your lodger moves out you should return the security deposit paid to you when they moved in. The only reasons you should withhold money are if there is damage to the room, property or contents, or any unpaid rent. If there has been any damage (beyond the expected wear and tear of someone living in a property) you will need to deduct a suitable amount to cover it. If you're not sure how much this will cost then say you'll find out and let them know – you should aim to do this within a week if possible.

UNPAID RENT

If your lodger owes you any rent when they move out you can deduct this from the deposit before returning it. Don't be tempted to let your lodger off the last month's rent and just keep the deposit – while this may seem like a good idea it doesn't leave you with any security if anything should happen in the last month.

PROBLEMS WITH YOUR LODGER

In the unlikely event you run into problems with your lodger you should try (in the first instance) to talk to them. Chapter 6 *Living Together* includes plenty of advice (including some specific to living with a lodger). Most problems are the result of misunderstandings or a lack of communication and can be dealt with by talking to each other.

If problems persist then you, as the owner of the property (or the tenant if you rent), have more rights than your lodger. Your first resort should be to put everything in writing so there's a record of what the issues are and when you attempted to speak to the lodger about them. If you can't resolve your differences then you should give your lodger notice to leave (again in writing as well as verbally), as set out in your agreement. If things aren't working out your lodger will probably be as happy to move out as you are to see them go. The standard notice period is 28 days. In extreme circumstances (such as abusive or violent behaviour, drug taking or other criminal activity) you can give a shorter notice period.

EVICTION

In the worst case scenario you could end up with a lodger to whom you have given notice but refuses to leave. This is an extremely difficult situation and should be handled carefully – luckily this rarely happens. After giving your lodger the required notice period (after which they still haven't left) you will need to change the locks once they're out and not allow them entry into the property. This is an extreme course of action and should only be taken where absolutely necessary. We'd recommend seeking some legal advice before you attempt this – in part to protect yourself against any comeback if you fail to follow all the necessary legal procedures. Contact Shelter or Citizens Advice to talk things through before you attempt a forcible eviction.

Checklist

Having decided to take in a lodger you'll need to plan ahead, so here's our step by step guide to help you work your way through the process with minimal fuss and make sure you've got everything covered in advance.

Points marked with an asterisk (*) are absolutely essential – you shouldn't ignore any of these. Those with the 'recommended' symbol ® are points we'd strongly advise you to consider.

This list can be downloaded and printed from: www.SpareRoom.co.uk/ essentialguide/lodger.

1*   Check with your mortgage lender, landlord or local authority

2*   Inform your insurance provider

3*   Inform your local benefits agency

4*   Let the council know if you're paying reduced council tax for single occupancy.

5®   Get the room ready

6®   Decide in advance what the terms and conditions will be

7®   Get a lodger agreement

8®   Check local rents

9*   Get your gas appliances checked by a Gas Safe registered professional

10®   Advertise your room

11®   Viewings

12®   Credit checks

13®   Signing contracts, deposit and agreeing terms and conditions

14®   Getting your lodger to set up a standing order for the rent

15®   Lodger moves in

16*   Inform your tax office if you earn over £4,250

From one live-in landlord to another

Most people find taking in a lodger a positive experience. Even those who have had difficulties with a lodger often put it down to bad luck and try again, usually with better results. Don't forget, it's not just about how good the lodger is, it's also about how you are as a landlord and that's something you'll become better at as you progress.

We asked a selection of live-in landlords who use SpareRoom to give us their tips for anyone new to taking in lodgers. Here's a selection of their experiences and advice.

'I have had four lodgers and all have been totally different. None of them have really integrated as I thought but, as time has gone on, I actually preferred it that way. I find the best lodger is one that has a job and hobbies so they don't feel caged in the house. My only tip would be don't believe everything they tell you (e.g "I'm really clean and tidy"). Speak to previous landlords to check.'

'I have had two lodgers now. The requirements of the first were very different to the second so you can't prepare totally for what you think a person will need. Be flexible. Also treat your lodger as part of the family: trust and respect hopefully will be returned.'

'I have had good and bad experiences and have learned to trust my instinct about a person and be upfront about expectations.'

'I recommend the "boyfriend" rule that overnight guests can stay for as many nights as the lodger stays at theirs.'

'Set the ground rules from the outset – we could have failed miserably as housemates because neither of us had been in this position before. However, we agreed to start again, established the ground rules and things have been good ever since.'

'I have realised that lots of my preconceptions about the type of lodger I thought I would like were wrong. As it turns out, I'm not sure that friendship is the key, but rather that there are clear boundaries that are respected in each direction. My current lodger is someone whom I like very much and have a great deal of respect for, and am more than happy to share my home with, but with whom I have no personal relationship at all. After all, it is a business arrangement. My first lodger and I shared a lot in common in terms of interests, as I had advertised in this way. But in fact this caused quite a strain as it was then hard to keep the right distance.'

'I have found it much easier to have a lodger live with me than I thought it would be. It's best to lay out what you expect of them right from the start – if there is anything you are unhappy with bring it up straight away but in a calm and reasonable way. I have only had one difficulty, quickly resolved, and would consider another lodger should my current lodger decide to move on.'

'I have always had great people from SpareRoom – with one exception. My own fault – I allowed myself to be rushed into saying he could take the room, even though I had lots of reservations. My advice to everyone is, don't be rushed into a decision.'

'Getting a random person in is completely different to living with a friend and, unless you're exceptionally chilled-out, small things will bug you, it's only human. The key is to be tolerant and understanding and just talk – don't rely on emails or texts to communicate. Make sure you share out the household chores too, or get a (good) cleaner, as this can be the cause of so many little bug-bears that needn't be there.'

'Our lodgers generally do Monday to Friday and that works well for us as we are a family with two young boys. I wouldn't say that the lodgers become friends but we usually have a relaxed, friendly relationship with our lodgers. At the end of the day they are paying for a room so it is a commercial relationship, but we have usually found that is it quite amicable and if it doesn't work then we ask them to move out.'

'It took three attempts but have finally found someone I get on with and we both seem to get on living together. It can be difficult and is a lot to get used to but I don't regret it.'

'Don't take anything for granted. If you haven't shared for a while you forget that other people can live in very different ways! Don't assume anything. Everything needs to be communicated, whether you prefer to do this verbally or on paper, even down to who puts the rubbish out and locking the back door. I have a lovely lodger and think I have been rather lucky. I would communicate more the next time – we are quite relaxed but it could have been very different.'

'Most lodgers are very good. In 28 years of letting my rooms I have only had to ask two to leave – one was very weird and the other one was just smelly. I must have had hundreds by now so thats a very good percentage – about a quarter became good friends.'

'Having done this for a few years I would say that a combination of trustworthiness and a good personality are the most important things. Always go with your instincts and you'll be fine. If there's any doubt then there is no doubt.'

'I just make sure I meet and really feel out the prospective tenant before agreeing. I never "close" on the first impression, saying I have a couple more people to see still, then review my feelings afterwards. If they're negative I politely decline the guest. I saw three or four people each time before taking my lodgers.'

'Most have been okay but one did not pay his rent. He kept saying there had been some problem at the bank. Stupidly I believed him and then he disappeared, having paid one month's rent out of three. Don't let this put you off though – my current lodger has become a true friend.'

'It has been a good experience for me, apart from the odd blip which was quickly sorted out. I have always been straight with people and ask them to regard the house as their home, treat it with respect, and just do things off their own back if they see something needs doing rather than have a list of "duties". On the whole they have been more responsible if they know it is up to them. I just have to mention a few points occasionally and I try to lead by example (e.g. always leave the kitchen clean and put everything in the dishwasher or wash and put it away after cooking my meal or empty the dishwasher when it is finished). The lodgers are responsible for keeping their bathroom clean – they share a bathroom and have their rooms on the same floor. It has been a good experience for me on the whole but when there are problems you just have to make it clear that it is not acceptable. I can be authoritative if I need to be but usually we chat comfortably, get on well, they tell me their problems sometimes but I still think it is good to keep a little distance.'

'I have had seven lodgers in the last few years, one for over three years who had already been a friend. Personally I think it's easier on the finance side to have people you do not know, however, on the comfort side, knowing your lodgers can be a great deal more fun and relaxing. Your choice depends how you live and how well you think you can integrate a stranger into your home.'

'Know what kind of person you want and then interview prospective lodgers thoroughly to ensure you get a good match. We've had several and, as we've got better at interviewing them, the experience has got more comfortable.'

CHAPTER FIVE
The Language of Flatsharing

Flatshare adverts have their own language and terminology so it's important to know what it all means, especially if you're new to the UK. Some terms that are widely used in one country may mean something slightly different in another (see 'Room mate' for an example of this).

In the days of rooms being advertised in local newspapers, jargon and abbreviations such as GCH (gas central heating) were invented to make it easier to fit more words into an advert. Some of these still exist today but there are also plenty more terms you'll come across in your search.

Here's a list of the more commonly used ones.

Administration fee
This is a fee, usually payable to an agent (see below), to cover the drawing up of contracts or the checking of references.

Agent
An agent manages part or all of the process of finding tenants for a landlord in exchange for a fee. This may mean simply finding tenants but could also extend to conducting viewings, arranging contracts and even managing the property during the tenancy.

Assured short-hold tenancy (AST)
This is the most common form of tenancy in the UK and is similar to an assured tenancy but lasts for a fixed period of at least six months. ASTs are more popular as they make it easier for the landlord to give notice and end the agreement.

Assured tenancy

An assured tenancy gives you the right to remain in a property unless the landlord can convince the court there are good reasons to evict you (such as rent arrears, damage etc.).

Bedsit

Bedsit (an abbreviation of 'bed sitting room') refers to single room accommodation that serves as both a bedroom and living space in one. Generally, you'll be sharing a bathroom and/or kitchen with others.

Bills included

This means utilities such as gas, electricity and water are included in the rent. Council tax and other bills such as phone or broadband may be included but check in advance which bills are covered, as 'bills included' is fairly non-specific.

Buddy up

Buddy Ups are a feature found on sites like SpareRoom.co.uk and at speed flatmating events. They allow individual room seekers (or groups of seekers) to join together to find a property.

Bungalow

A bungalow is a single-storey house with all the rooms on the ground floor.

Buy-to-let

This term is used to describe buying a property with the specific intention of renting it out rather than living in it. Buy-to-let has been extremely popular in recent years as, until recently, house prices were rising and mortgages were relatively easy to get.

Buy-to-share

This describes the increasing trend of buying a property with the intention of renting out one or more rooms to help pay the mortgage whilst living in it yourself. Some lenders offer specialist mortgages for this, although you'll be hard pressed to find one at the moment.

Co-buying

Co-buying refers to buying with another person who isn't your partner, generally in order to be able to buy property you couldn't otherwise afford.

Contents insurance

A policy covering your personal possessions, clothes, furniture and other belongings as opposed to buildings insurance, which covers the structure itself. Generally, if you're renting or sharing you'll need to get your own contents insurance as it won't be included in the rent. See also 'Room contents insurance'.

Contract

A contract, in the world of flatsharing, refers to a written agreement between the tenant(s) and landlord, signed by both parties, setting out the terms of the tenancy. It's always a good idea to have an agreement of some kind as it protects both the tenant and the landlord. See also 'Tenancy agreement'. For information on the main types of contract see Chapter 8, *Contracts, Rights and Agreements*.

Conversion

A conversion is a house that has been divided to make two or more flats. Often there will be a communal entrance with individual front doors off the main hallway. Victorian conversions are amongst the most popular flats in the UK, especially for buyers.

Cottage

The term cottage generally refers to smaller rural properties, although it can be used for other properties (usually if the person describing the property wants to convey a sense of quaintness or cosiness).

Council tax

Council tax is a form of property tax based on the value of a property and (to some extent) who lives in it. Council tax raises around 25% of local government revenue in Great Britain.

Credit check

Landlords and agents may carry out a credit check to satisfy themselves that you can afford to pay your rent before allowing you to move in. This may involve contacting your bank or employer to verify your income.

Deposit

A deposit is a fixed sum taken by landlords or letting agents at the start of a tenancy to cover reasonable losses (such as rent arrears or damage beyond the normal wear and tear of living in a property). Whether you're renting or lodging, you should expect to pay a deposit before moving in; the standard amount is one month's rent. Providing you don't owe any rent at the end of your tenancy, and haven't caused any damage, your deposit should be refunded in full by your landlord. See also 'Tenancy deposit scheme' below.

Detached

A detached house is one that is completely separate from its neighbours, as opposed to terraced or semi-detached houses, which are connected by a shared wall.

Double room

This applies to the size of the room and means a room that has, or can fit, a double bed. In practical terms, the size of double rooms offered varies a great deal – some have just enough space for a double bed and for you to squeeze round it while others will have plenty of space.

DSS

DSS refers to anyone who relies on state benefits to pay their rent. The term comes from the abbreviation of 'Department for Social Security'. You will often see room adverts with the term 'no DSS', meaning the room isn't available to those on benefits.

En-suite

An en-suite room is one that has its own bathroom or toilet, for sole use of that room's occupant.

Eviction

Eviction refers to the process of a landlord expelling a tenant from a property before the end of an agreed term. This is governed by strict rules dependent on the kind of tenancy in place. For information on eviction, see Chapter 8.

Ex-local authority

This refers to a property formerly owned (and usually built) by the council. Often, especially in London, this refers to purpose built blocks of flats.

Fixed term

This refers to the length of an assured shorthold tenancy. If, at the end of the period, you remain in the property without signing a new fixed term agreement, the tenancy becomes periodic (see page 82).

Flat

A flat is usually a property occupying only part of a building – known as an apartment in the US. Blocks of flats can be purpose built or in converted houses.

Flatmate

Flatmate is a term mainly used in the UK and Australia to describe someone who shares a flat or apartment with you. Generally, housemate is used when the property is a house but both terms are fairly interchangeable.

Flatshare

This describes a property (usually a flat) shared by one or more (generally unrelated) people when each person (or couple) has their own bedroom. See also 'Houseshare'.

Fractional letting

Fractional letting is a term used to describe ongoing lettings that don't cover the whole week. The most common example is Monday–Friday lets where the tenant is elsewhere for weekends. Fractional lets are a good way of taking in a lodger without them being there all the time and provide a useful solution for those who commute long distances to work but want to maintain a home elsewhere.

Garden flat

Literally a flat with a garden.

Granny flat

A granny flat is a smaller, self-contained flat at the back or on an upper floor of the main property, usually with its own front door. The term comes from people creating a separate space for an older relative to live with the family without being in the main house.

HMO

HMO is the new buzzword in property rental. It stands for Home in Multiple Occupation and is a system used by local authorities to regulate the quality and safety of shared accommodation. Rules apply to determine what is and isn't an HMO and only certain properties require a licence. If you're renting out a room to a single lodger then you needn't worry about this but for more information, see Chapter 8 or have a look at: www.HMO.org.uk.

House

This usually refers to a whole property on more than one level. One house can contain several flats.

Houseboat

A houseboat is a floating house usually, but not always, converted from a boat.

House rules

The house rules are a set of written or verbal terms agreed upon by all housemates and designed to divide responsibility. They can range from essentials, such as how much rent each housemate pays, to things like who is responsible for cleaning what and how often. House rules aren't essential but can help everyone understand what's expected and minimize conflict.

Houseshare, house share

This describes a property (usually a house) shared by one or more (generally unrelated) people when each person (or couple) has their own bedroom. See also 'Flatshare'.

Inter-sharer agreement

This is similar in some ways to the house rules (see above). An inter-sharer agreement is a contract between housemates which (usually) deals with the more important aspects of the share, such as rent and bills.

Inventory

Some landlords/agents ask tenants to sign an inventory at the same time as their contract. This is a list of all the fixtures and fittings (including furniture) in the room and their current condition. Always check carefully and report any mistakes or omissions BEFORE signing. Once signed, this document provides proof to protect both the tenant and the landlord when inspecting the room on moving out. The inventory will usually be consulted before you get your deposit returned in full so, while it may seem like just another piece of paper when you move in, it's important to check it thoroughly. For more on inventories, see Chapter 8.

Joint and several

A joint and several agreement is one which holds all parties liable. This means if one housemate fails to pay, the landlord can chase any one of the tenants to recover the money. For more information, see Chapter 8.

Key (or card) meter

In rental properties it is common for gas and electricity to be supplied via a key or card meter. This works as a 'pay as you go' system that prevents tenants from running up big utility bills before leaving a property. The downside is generally higher energy prices for key meter customers. For more on this, see Chapter 7.

Landlord's insurance

This is a specific type of insurance offered by certain companies to cover the needs of landlords and can cover anything from rent losses and damage to re-housing tenants in the case of emergencies.

Live-in landlord

A homeowner who rents out one or more rooms in their property whilst living there themselves (i.e. has one or more lodgers) is referred to as a live-in landlord.

Live-out landlord

This refers to a landlord who rents a property they do not live in themselves.

Lodger

A lodger is a tenant who rents a room (or rooms) in another person's house, usually from a live-in landlord (see above). Lodgers' arrangements vary greatly from simply sharing the property with the landlord to living with a family and having meals provided. For more on this, see Chapter 4.

Loft apartment

Generally in former industrial premises, and often open plan in layout, loft apartments have high ceilings and lots of natural light. New York is famous for its loft apartments, popular with artists in the 1960s and 70s and highly desirable (and therefore expensive) now.

Maisonette

A flat on two levels with internal stairs and/or it's own street-level front door is known as a maisonette. These can be purpose built or converted by dividing an existing house.

Mansion

A mansion is usually a very large or expensive house. The term is also used in London to describe a particular style of purpose built flats which generally have high ceilings.

Master bedroom

The biggest bedroom in a property is usually referred to as the master bedroom.

Mews

Mews are traditionally rows of former stables now converted into residential properties. The original ground floor stable area is usually a garage and the living quarters (which would have housed the ostler) are above. Traditional mews houses in London were built behind larger houses so the owners could have their horses (and staff) close by, as a result they're nearly always found in wealthier areas. The term is also used to describe rows of modern properties that mimic the mews style of construction (and is generally used to add desirability to the properties, as mews houses are highly sought after).

Mon–Fri renting

This is a arrangement where the room to let is only available Monday to Friday. This can be a good option for commuters who stay in the city during the week but go home for weekends as rent is reduced accordingly. It can also a good option for the person renting out the room as they get the property to themselves at weekends. See also 'Fractional letting', page 77.

No DSS

This means that the room is not available to those reliant on state benefits to pay their rent.

Party wall

The wall shared by two connected properties, for example terraced houses, is referred to as a party wall.

PCM

This stands for per calendar month so means the rent is calculated as a monthly amount, usually payable at the start of each month.

Penthouse

The penthouse is the top floor of a multi-storey building and is generally the most desirable flat in taller buildings due to improved views, no upstairs neighbours and a greater distance from street noise.

Periodic tenancy

A periodic tenancy is one without a fixed term, usually the result of a fixed-term tenancy that has expired. If you have a periodic tenancy your landlord may not need a reason to ask you to leave.

Postcode

The system used by the Royal Mail in the UK to condense address information into a simple formula (as the US postal service does with zip codes). For more information, see Chapter 2, *Find a Flatshare* – for information on London postcodes, see Chapter 9.

Purpose built

This refers to a collection of flats built as such rather than those converted from an existing building.

PW

PW stands for per week, meaning the rent is payable every seven days.

References

References are a set of documents recommending you as a suitable tenant. The most common form is a letter of recommendation from your previous landlord but you may also be asked for references from your bank and employer. It's common to see the phrase 'references required' in room listings.

Rent a Room Scheme

The Rent a Room Scheme is a government incentive that allows you to earn up to £4,250 a year tax-free by taking in a lodger. The scheme is becoming very popular as more people look to take in lodgers to help with their mortgage payments.

Re-signing fee

Some agents and landlords are happy to extend your contract at the end of the agreed term or amend a contract to include a new flatmate, but you'll usually have to sign a new agreement. Many agents charge a fee for this.

Room contents insurance

Room contents insurance is a specific policy to cover those who rent a room within a property. The policy will insure all your personal belongings without you having to have shared contents insurance for the whole property (for more information and links to insurance providers, see Chapter 7, *Finance and Bills*).

Roommate

Roommate is an American term, now used internationally due to the influence of American film and TV. As the name suggests it can be use to describe someone who shares a room with you but is often used as we would use 'flatmate', to describe people who share a flat or house with you (i.e. they don't have to be in the same room to be described as a roommate). In the UK 'roommate' would generally mean someone you share a room with.

Room seeker

Room seeker is the term used to describe someone who is looking for accommodation in a shared property or with a live-in landlord.

Seasonal lettings

Seasonal lets are short-term lets covering a particular time of year (such as summer or the duration of a particular event). For example, many people in Edinburgh rent out a room during the annual Edinburgh Festival as thousands of people visit the city every year either to attend or perform at the festival, so it's a good chance to make some money without having a permanent lodger.

Semi or semi-detached

This refers to two houses joined together by a connecting wall (as opposed to detached houses).

Sharers

Sharers is the term used to describe those living in shared accommodation together. Usually sharers is used to refer to people renting a whole property between them but can apply to any group of people who share accommodation.

Short-term let

A short-term let is one that lasts for three months or less. Standard tenancies are usually six months and above so anything under that could be considered short term.

Single room

This denotes a room with space for a single bed rather than a double.

Speed Flatmating®

Speed Flatmating is a social event, run by SpareRoom.co.uk, and is popular in London as a way to meet several potential flatmates in one evening. See Chapter 9 or: www.speedflatmating.co.uk for more information.

Studio or studio flat

A single room for cooking, living and sleeping with its own bathroom is called a studio flat. The room is usually divided into a cooking area and a living/sleeping area and is, in basic terms, a one-bed flat without the bedroom.

Sub-let

A sub-let is an arrangement whereby the existing tenant lets all or part of the property to another. This is a complicated issue and one we usually advise people to avoid – see Chapter 1, *Types of Let*, for more information on this subject.

Tenancy agreement

A tenancy agreement is a contract (verbal or written but usually written) between landlord and tenant. The contract outlines the rights both parties have (for example, your right to occupy the property and the landlord's right to receive rent from you). The contract is designed to protect both the tenant and the landlord and will contain information on issues such as whether you can keep pets in the property and how much notice you need to give if you want to leave. See also 'Contract', or, for further information, see Chapter 8, *Contracts, Rights and Agreements*.

Tenancy Deposit Scheme

The Tenancy Deposit Scheme was introduced by the government in 2007 to safeguard deposits taken by landlords. So far the scheme only applies to assured shorthold tenancies (see above) and requires the landlord to place the deposit in one of a choice of schemes to be returned in full at the end of the tenancy (provided there's no unpaid rent or damage to be paid for). If there's a dispute about the amount of deposit to be returned then there's help available to sort out the problem in a fair manner. See Chapter 8 for more on the scheme.

Tenant

Someone who rents and occupies a property from another is known as a tenant (unless they live with their landlord, in which case they become a lodger).

Terraced house

A terraced house is one in a row of (usually) identical properties connected to each other by shared (or 'party') walls.

Townhouse

This term is used to describe a style of (originally) upper class house (generally in London), often with three or more floors.

Viewing

This is the term for showing someone round (or being shown round) a property.

Walk-up flat

Walk-up refers to a block of flats (mostly low rise) that have individual front doors externally, usually off a shared walkway (as opposed to off a communal internal hallway).

Interlude: Fighting Over the Remote – Flatshare on the Box

Over the years there have been many memorable films and TV shows based around flatshares and lodgers. Some of these are classics and some not so great, but all recognize that there's a wealth of humour, fun, sadness, conflict and drama (all the things we need for a good story) in any shared house or flat.

Here are a few of our favourites.

Film

SHALLOW GRAVE

Set in Edinburgh, the film opens with a group of friends interviewing potential candidates to fill their spare room, in what is probably the most memorable flatshare scene ever written. If you've ever been to look round a shared flat then this is the interview you least want.

The high (or possibly low) point – certainly the funniest – comes when Alex Law (played by Ewan McGregor in his first main feature role) asks one hopeful:

> So tell me, Cameron, just tell me because I'd like to know, what on earth could make you think that we would want to share a flat like this with someone like you? I mean, my first impression, and they're rarely wrong, is that you have none of the qualities that we normally seek in a prospective flatmate.

The plot begins to unfold once chosen flatmate Hugo (Keith Allen) moves in and promptly dies, at which point the flatmates discover a huge amount of cash in his room. Should you ever find yourself in this situation (and we hope you don't), we'd suggest you go to the police rather than following their example!

SINGLE WHITE FEMALE

This 1992 thriller starring Jennifer Jason Leigh and Bridget Fonda takes us to the extremes of what can go wrong when you let a stranger into your home. Allie Jones needs a new flatmate to replace the fiancé she's kicked out but starts to despair after a string of unsuitable candidates apply. Then along comes Hedy Carlson, who Allie decides is perfect and gives the room to. As the film unfolds, and Hedy starts becoming unnervingly like Allie, we discover the truth about her background and she turns out to be far from the ideal flatmate.

The film's tagline, 'Allie's new roommate is about to borrow a few things without asking. Her clothes. Her boyfriend. Her life' sums up all that people worry about when they have to find a new flatmate. Luckily it generally doesn't end like this!

THE ODD COUPLE

Felix (Jack Lemon) has split up with his wife and decides to kill himself but is saved by Oscar (Walter Matthau). Oscar persuades Felix to move in with him but it turns out they have very different ideas of how they'd like to live. Neil Simon was nominated for an Oscar for the screenplay, based on his own Broadway play. A TV series based on the play was also a hit in the 70s.

TV

THE YOUNG ONES

This classic sitcom, based on four very different characters sharing student digs in 1980s Britain, made stars of actors Rik Mayall (who also co-wrote the series), Adrian Edmonson and Nigel Planer (and co-writer Ben Elton). The students' slapstick, violent and often downright surreal adventures were a breath of fresh air when they first hit UK TV screens and helped give rise to the wave of 'alternative comedy' which swept Britain in the 1980s.

The show was far more violent, dirty and anarchic than anything previously seen in a prime time comedy slot on the BBC and, at times, it seemed like the plot was non-existent, but the show was a huge hit with audiences and ran for 26 episodes between 1982 and 1985.

RISING DAMP

Another all-time classic UK sitcom, this time set in a seedy bedsit house run by thoroughly unpleasant landlord Rigsby (played by Leonard Rossiter). The series (which later spawned a film) was based on Eric Chappell's play *The Banana Box*, which originally starred Wilfred Bramble as the landlord (who was called Rooksby, later changed to Rigsby after complaints from a real life Mr Rooksby) before Rossiter took over. Bramble is best known for playing another cantankerous old miser Albert Steptoe in the classic sitcom *Steptoe and Son*, as well as Paul McCartney's grandfather ('he's very clean') in *A Hard Day's Night*. In fact, of the show's regular cast, only Richard Beckinsale hadn't already played his part in the stage version.

Rigsby remains, for many, the stereotypical image of the money-grabbing landlord, presiding over a kingdon of shabby little bedsits, long after the world of bedsits and lodgers has moved on.

MEN BEHAVING BADLY

After the alternative comedy of *The Young Ones* in the 1980s, we had the laddism of *Men Behaving Badly* in the 1990s. The show, which was a huge hit for the BBC, actually started on ITV with Harry Enfield starring alongside Martin Clunes. Enfield quit after the first series and was replaced by Neil Morrissey but ITV lost faith, possibly feeling the show needed a star such as Enfield to guarantee ratings.

The BBC picked up the series in 1994 and took the decision to broadcast it after the 9 o'clock watershed, allowing the show to embrace its subject matter (and its humour, based on 'boobs, belching and booze') a little more directly.

Men Behaving Badly, whether the embracing lad culture of magazines such as *Loaded* or simply a backlash against the 90s caring, sharing 'new man' (as has been suggested), allowed audiences a glimpse into the life of two men struggling to grow up (and, often, failing to see why they should).

FRIENDS

The one where a group of six friends hang out in a New York coffee shop (and all seem to live with each other at some point).

Friends is probably the best loved (and most successful) sitcom of all time. Over the space of ten years (and ten seasons), the ups and downs of the relationships between Rachel, Ross, Monica, Joey, Chandler and Phoebe kept millions tuning in every week and made household names of the actors who portrayed them. It also spawned spin-off series *Joey* in which Matt Le Blanc's character moves to Hollywood in search of an acting career.

Friends shows a more contemporary view of flatsharing than either *The Young Ones* or *Rising Damp*. This type of shared accommodation, with groups of young professionals living together, is becoming far more common today (although most of us can't afford flats quite as nice as theirs).

The show won a whole host of awards, including several Emmys (most surprisingly one for Bruce Willis – Outstanding Guest Actor in a Comedy Series!).

PEEP SHOW

From the glamour of Manhattan to Apollo House, London Road, Croydon – BAFTA award winning series *Peep Show* follows the, generally frustrated, lives of two university friends sharing a flat. Mark (David Mitchell) is financially successful but socially awkward and generally pessimistic. Jeremy (Robert Webb) is far more socially confident and positive but has yet to achieve the recognition and success he believes he deserves.

The characters are mostly seen from their own point of view, or that of others (as opposed to that of the viewer) and the use of voiceover lets us know what they're thinking as well as what they're saying (a feature inspired by Woody Allen's use of subtitles in *Annie Hall*). Scenes are often filmed using cameras strapped to the actors' heads so we also get their visual perspective.

The show attracted a strong cult following when first broadcast by Channel 4 in 2003. By series three (in 2006) the series won the Best TV Comedy award at the British Comedy Awards (which it won again the following year, along with a Best TV Comedy Actor award for Mitchell).

Opera

Yes, believe it or not, there actually is a flatshare-based opera. Not only that, it's a good one!

LA BOHEME

Puccini's *La Boheme* follows the (mis)fortunes of a group of struggling artists living in a garret in Paris in the 1830s. The role of starving poet Rodolfo became one of Pavarotti's signature roles (despite it becoming more difficult over the years to imagine him as a starving anything) and his Act 1 aria *Che Gelida Manina* (generally known in English as *Your Tiny Hand is Frozen*) is one of the most popular and beautiful in all opera.

The opera is often referred to as part of the 'ABC of Opera' referring to *Aida, Boheme* and *Carmen*, three operas guaranteed to get bums on seats. When asked by Sir Thomas Beecham what his favourite opera was, King George V supposedly cited *La Boheme*. When asked why this was he replied 'Because it's the shortest'.

La Boheme was the basis for hit Broadway show *Rent*, and Baz Luhrmann's experience directing the opera for Opera Australia in 1990 must surely have had some influence on *Moulin Rouge*, which features a penniless writer, a Parisian garret and a dying heroine.

CHAPTER SIX
Living Together

Okay, so you've found the perfect room in a great flat and your flatmates seem lovely, all's well so far. Unfortunately it's not always as easy as this and, when a group of people live in close proximity to each other, there will be inevitable disputes and differences of opinion. We've all got our own needs when it comes to a place to live, some people prefer a busy, lively house whilst others need peace and quiet. You may be the kind of person who finds it impossible to relax until the washing up is done, whilst your friends don't mind a bit of mess as long as it gets sorted in the end.

According to SpareRoom.co.uk's users the things most likely to provoke an argument between housemates are cleanliness (56%) and noise levels (25%). In addition almost half of those in shared accommodation have argued at some point with their housemates about paying bills. Obviously when you're living with other people you won't always see eye to eye but there are certain problems which will inevitably crop up and steps you can take to avoid them before they do.

So, how do you move in without falling out? Some (if not most) of this may seem obvious but, despite the jokey nature of the advice, these really are some of the simplest things you can do to avoid annoying each other on a daily basis.

Cleanliness

Being next to godliness it's clear that cleanliness is likely to be a major source of conflict (we don't have any statistics on how many flatmates have argued about godliness but I'm guessing it's not the main source of disputes for most people). It stands to reason that any flatshare will only be as tidy as the untidiest person in it so if one of you is extremely houseproud and another is a slob you'll struggle to find the middle ground that's acceptable to both.

There are three main areas of any property that are going to be the obvious battlegrounds, they are:

- kitchen
- bathroom
- living room.

Each presents its own problems and likely trouble spots.

KITCHEN

This is the room with the potential to cause the most trouble, as it's the easiest to turn into a bombsite in minutes. Everyone will need to use the kitchen at some point (even the most committed non-cook will need to get to the kettle) and there's nothing worse than getting in after a day at work and having to wash up before you can cook.

The top trouble spots are:

Microwave

This is a simple one, if you've used the microwave to heat something and it's splattered all over (soup and porridge are best for this if you want a good example to try), clean it up after you've eaten. There's nothing worse than little stalactites of tomato soup hanging down from the roof of a microwave and, before too long, the whole thing will smell awful. There's also nothing quite like the smell of microwaved fish for staying power. A quick wipe down with a wet cloth will get rid of most of the mess, also, the glass plate you put things on is removable for a very good reason – so if you can clean it, do so.

Cooker

Similarly to the microwave an uncleaned cooker is no good to anyone. I'm certainly not suggesting you clean the whole thing every time you use it but wiping any spillages from the hob and cleaning the grill pan are simple basics you should become familiar with.

If anyone in the flat is vegetarian you should definitely clean anything you've used to cook meat as a matter of simple human decency.

Generally in any shared house the cooker will need a thorough scrub before you move out but it doesn't need to get so bad in the meantime that it sets off the smoke alarms every time you use the grill.

Fridge

The fridge is the classic image of flatshare neglect. With several people's food in there, and no one keen to throw someone else's stuff away, you can end up with mini civilizations living at the back. It'll be much easier if you buy essentials together so the fridge isn't full of half empty milk bottles, all of which are past their sell by date.

Spillages, drips and anything furry should be dealt with promptly. Milk that doesn't move when you shake the bottle can also be thrown out.

We saw a great invention in the Electrolux design competition last year, which isn't in production yet but certainly should be. It's called a Flatshare Fridge and consists of a stackable, modular set of mini fridges so you get one each and all disputes can be easily avoided. If someone else moves in you just get another module – fantastic! For a look at this simple work of genius just Google 'flatshare fridge' and you'll see what we mean.

Washing up

This is easy, wash up what you've used – it's really that simple. If you're cooking a big meal that requires loads of pots, pans and utensils then wash up as you go along so there are only a few bits left at the end. Everything else should be done soon after you've eaten so other people can use stuff. If you have a dishwasher then this all becomes easier, just pile everything in out of sight and stick a load on once it's full.

Remember, someone has to put the stuff back into cupboards at some point so the next lot of dirty dishes doesn't get added by someone who can't be bothered to see whether what's in there already is clean or not.

Matt says:

'I lived with a friend once who used to cook meals using everything in the kitchen then leave the washing up and go out for the night. As often as not he'd then stay with his girlfriend for a few days so I had to wash up everything before I could eat – no fun.'

Surfaces

Wipe 'em down, easy.

'One guy I lived with used to make coffee in a cafetiere. Somehow he always seemed to leave as much on the surfaces as in the mug and never cleaned up so we got into the habit of writing "clean this please" in the huge brown stains 'til he got the message. This method takes a little patience (or downright stubbornness) at first but works well in the long term.'

Steph

Bins

Empty the bins regularly and make sure you know what day rubbish collection is. Also, sort out your recycling but have a plan of what to do with it too, as there's no point separating it all if you're just going to chuck it in the bin eventually. Lots of supermarkets have recycling bins and more and more councils now collect recycling and provide special bins or boxes to put it in. Contact your local council to see if they provide a recycling collection service if you're not sure.

Bathroom

It shouldn't be that hard to keep a bathroom clean but it never quite manages to work that way. All that should be required is giving the bath a quick rinse after you use it and a more thorough clean every now and then, but there are a few other essentials:

Toilet

Use the toilet brush, that's what it's there for. Any unsightly marks left in the toilet need dealing with, nobody wants to see the consistency of your bowel movements (except Gillian McKeith and I'm guessing you don't live with her). Similarly, if you occasionally suffer from bad aim (I'm talking to you here boys, girls really have to work hard to miss), clean it up. Don't just leave it there and, if questioned, say you must have dripped a bit of water from the sink washing your hands – this is what kids do and we know they're lying so you won't get away with it.

If you've created a new and unusual atmosphere after using the toilet (made it stink basically) it's not okay to just come out and proudly declare 'I wouldn't go in there for a while if I were you'. Open a window, strike a match or (better still) keep a scented candle in there for such occasions. Air freshener is no good, a strong smell of poo is unpleasant, a strong smell of poo with a thick veneer of air freshener is truly horrendous.

Matt says:

'Always (ALWAYS) replace a toilet roll if you finish one and don't squeeze the toothpaste from the top of the tube so it all stays at the end – these are the things which set us above apes. I volunteered at a monkey sanctuary once and never saw a single monkey replace a toilet roll.'

Bath

A quick rinse not only gets rid of soap scum and cleans the bath but also deals with any stray 'intimate' hairs you may have left and which I can guarantee none of your flatmates wants to find floating past their navel when they use the bath after you.

Living room

This is a truly shared space, as you'll spend most of your time as a group here, so keep it tidy. When it comes to your own stuff being left in the living room there's a simple rule to follow; if others will want to use it regularly and you don't mind this then fine, otherwise it lives in your own room.

Examples of stuff you can leave in the living room:

TV/DVD player/stereo/games console

If there isn't one of these in the property already and you have one you're happy to share, then great. Beware of falling into the 'it's my TV so we'll watch whatever I say we will' trap though as this isn't friendly and will cancel out any good will created by leaving your TV in the living room in the first place.

Magazines

If you've read these and think other people may want to then fine; don't just use the living room as a dumping ground though.

Books/DVDs/CDs

Things like this are always good to share but don't just keep all your belongings in the living room because you don't want to clutter up your own room. Also be aware that not everyone has the same attitude to your stuff as you do. If you expect discs to be put back in the correct cases and books to be read without the pages having their corners bent over and the spine broken then maybe you should keep them in your room and lend out at your discretion.

Examples of things you should find somewhere else to put:

Last night's socks

Take them off if you want but don't leave them on the floor for days (or even overnight) as the chance of someone else wanting to use them is fairly slim.

All your shoes

I don't really need to tell you this, do I?

Your bike

Or this, surely?

Your best mate who came for the weekend and is still on the sofa five days later

Friends come and go but, having come, they do need to go at some point.

Washing

If you've done a load of washing and left it on radiators, or in the living room, to dry you should put it away once it is dry. This is partly so your flatmates can use the space to dry their clothes and partly because nobody wants to eat their dinner with a radiator full of someone else's pants watching them.

Noise levels

Noise can prove one of the most intrusive elements of living with other people – even noise from neighbours above, below or sideways can really prove troublesome. In a shared house this is magnified, as you're likely to have more TV, more music, more hairdryers and more conversations going on all at once.

A basic level of noise is inevitable in any shared house but there are a few points worth looking at if you want a happy harmonious household.

PARTIES

It's always a good idea to check with everyone in the house before inviting loads of people over. If you're all happy with this it's probably also worth warning your neighbours in advance (and maybe dropping in a bottle of wine the day after as a thank you for their tolerance). Often people don't mind a bit of noise every now and then, as long as it's not all the time and you have the manners to warn them. You could even invite your neighbours to come along if you get on okay with them.

Sharer's tip:
'I live in a shared house in South East London with four other people. We're not a regular party house but do like to have the odd get together now and then and, when we do, they can go on a bit! Our next door neighbours are a lovely couple in their 80s who have lived in the area for 40 years, we always invite them to pop in for a drink if we're having a party and they generally do. On New Year's Eve they came at 11pm and stayed 'til 1.30! Having a good relationship with them means we can make a bit of noise now and then and they don't mind, or feel intimidated by it, as they know us.'

Gemma

MUSIC

With several rooms (and several people wanting to listen to their own music all at the same time) things can get a bit chaotic in a shared house. The first thing to remember is that loud music is not a challenge – it's generally better to get someone to turn their music down, shut the door or buy some headphones than decide you'll drown them out.

If someone repeatedly plays loud music (especially really early or really late) your options generally involve having a word or putting up with it. You should at least do your flatmate the courtesy of talking to them about it instead of second guessing their reaction. If they really won't turn it down then at least they'll know it bothers you and you'll know they're making a conscious choice to be loud. Often people won't realize how obtrusive their music is until you tell them.

Time of day

With any kind of noise (music, TV, hoovering, using your noisy juicer) it's always best not to start too early or go on too late. You run the risk of annoying your flatmates and your neighbours (especially if they have children who go to bed early just on the other side of your bedroom wall).

Remember that things don't have to be that loud to be annoying, the subwoofer of a surround sound speaker set can really rattle the windows a floor up or down without it seeming loud at all to you.

Money and bills

Sort out as much in advance as you can, money has the potential to become a real flashpoint for arguments so the less you leave until there's a problem the better. See Chapter 7, *Finance and Bills*, for advice on this.

Space and privacy

Everyone needs a bit of space of their own, unfortunately not everyone is so good at recognizing this fact in others. Luckily, in these days of mobile phones and wi-fi, it's at least possible to make phone calls and check your emails in peace without having to talk quietly so everyone else in the room can watch *Eastenders*.

PARTNERS

In any shared house space can become an issue, especially if partners become involved. If your flatmates have partners who regularly stay over then it's even harder to use the bathroom in the morning and things can get hectic. This can be fine if you all get on but, if things aren't that harmonious to start with, all out war can soon begin.

It might be an idea to limit the number of nights people can have their partners over to stay, as having an extra person there all the time can get a bit much, especially if they end up practically living with you.

> 'I moved into a four-bed flat with three of my mates a few years ago; after about a month one of their girlfriends came down for the weekend and didn't leave for six months! It meant we all had an extra flatmate who didn't contribute anything to the bills or rent and spent hours every day in the bathroom. Nobody said anything for the first few weeks and, after that, it became too late to do anything about it.'
>
> Edward

LOCKS AND CLOSING YOUR DOOR

Having locks on your bedroom doors in a shared house can be really useful, especially if you don't know the other housemates when you move in. The problem is, in locking your door to the people you live with, you're basically saying 'I don't trust you completely'. It may stop everyone borrowing your belongings though so what you do with locks is really up to you in the end.

If you have room contents insurance (see Chapter 7) then your policy may require you to have a lock on your bedroom door (and use it while you're out) in which case it's a good idea. It's probably a good idea to lock your room if you'll be away for a few days anyway, though your housemates may well want to use your room for guests while you're away so this in itself may become problematic.

The case of the flatmate and the alleged sister

'I shared a two-bed flat with one of my best friends for a couple of years. One weekend I was due to be away and he asked if it was okay for him to use my room as his sister was coming down for the weekend. He offered her his bed and slept in mine, which seemed best seeing as I didn't even know her. This worked so well that he only ever invited her down while I was away so, in two years of living together, she visited six or seven times and we never met.

   I did wonder if she really existed until a few years later when I met her at my friend's wedding!'

Tom

Conflict

Conflict and arguments are bound to feature in any kind of shared accommodation at some stage. There are things you can do to reduce conflict but, every so often, that just won't be possible and you'll have to deal with it. Most people tend to conform to one of the two following types when faced with conflict:

- aggressive
- passive.

Being aggressive looks, at first sight, like you're tackling the problem head on but (more often than not) aggressive behaviour won't sort out a problem and can make things far worse incredibly quickly.

A passive response to conflict will buy you a little time in the short term (and generally won't raise tempers even further straight away). The trouble is it doesn't deal with the problem, it also allows everyone time to go away and go over things on their own and come up with yet more reasons why they're hard done by in this particular instance.

The only real option for dealing with conflict is to talk it through. This can be extremely daunting, especially if you're dealing with someone who becomes aggressive when confronted.

BE BRAVE, BE HONEST

In sitting down to talk through a conflict you've already shown a certain amount of bravery and, even better, a willingness to resolve the problem. Once you're round the table and ready to talk (and hopefully listen) you've got the best chance you'll get to work out your differences. Make sure you're honest about how you feel without straying too much into the territory of blame – if you can say exactly what the problem is, as far as you're concerned, then you're part way there. Try and avoid thinking that the problem is entirely of your housemate's making unless you're 100% certain that's the case.

DON'T JUST TALK – LISTEN

Having the chance to get whatever's bothering you off your chest shouldn't prevent you from letting the other person have their say. If you go into the conversation determined to prove yourself right at all costs you're not giving it a chance to work. You've (hopefully) been honest about how you feel, let the other person (or persons) do the same.

TREAT THE PROCESS (AND THE OTHER PERSON) WITH RESPECT

If you can go into the conversation presuming the other person has the best of intentions and wants to resolve the conflict you'll stand a better chance of dealing with each other with respect. If you both go in looking to be proved right and waiting for the comment you can be justifiably indignant about, then you're missing the point. Surely neither of you really wants tension and arguments?

DO YOUR BEST NOT TO LOSE YOUR TEMPER

However wound up and unfairly treated you feel, try not to lose your temper. If necessary ask for a bit of time to cool off (whether this is ten minutes to make a coffee or walk round the block, or 24 hours). Losing your cool will only allow the other person to respond in kind and feel justified in doing so. The same applies to language.

WATCH YOUR LANGUAGE

Try not to use offensive language (even if the, normally civil, conversations you have with the other person are generally full of swear words and neither of you minds). Using bad language directed at something or someone else (the football on TV, for example) isn't quite the same as having bad language directed at you. If in doubt, leave it out (I'm not sure why all pithy bits of advice have to rhyme but they always seem to – Matt).

COMMUNICATION – LEAVING NOTES

Flat and house shares seem to be the only places in the world where it's considered acceptable (even desirable) to conduct conversations via post-it notes stuck on a fridge. You wouldn't solve a problem at work like this so it's unlikely you'll convince your flatmate of their unreasonable behaviour in this fashion either.

The fridge note works (on one level) for two reasons:

- In most flatshares not everyone will be around at the same time so some form of time delayed communication can be handy.
- Everyone uses the fridge at some point.

It doesn't work for several more:

- Tone of voice is absent so it's hard to judge intent – something may be read as a dig which isn't intended that way.
- Writing something down is a very permanent way of saying something you may have only thought for two seconds.
- The notes are left where everyone can see them so the conversation becomes public.
- Notes end up getting written at times when you're not best able to judge tone and content (such as at midnight when you've finally managed to get your key in the door and have stumbled into the kitchen looking for bread to toast/burn and someone has finished off the last few slices).

Try and resist the impulse to communicate through leaving notes unless all other forms of communication have already broken down.

I got into a note war with my flatmate

'We ended up not speaking to each other as we didn't get on, so left notes for each other about house stuff. The notes ended up getting more and more nasty until we had to sort it out (three weeks before we moved out into separate flatshares).'

Sarah

For a hugely entertaining look at fridge communication in flatshares, get a copy of Oonagh O'Hagan's *I Lick My Cheese and Other Notes From the Frontline of Flat-Sharing* (Sphere, 2007).

House rules

While it may seem a bit over the top, it's worth considering a set of house rules so you avoid the majority of arguments before they happen. It's entirely up to you what you include (and you don't have to write them down and pin them up in the kitchen), but a quick discussion about how you all expect things to be in the house when you first move in may well save a serious argument a few months down the line.

Basic things to consider including in the house rules might be:

- what shopping (if any) you're going to buy together
- how you're going to sort out paying the bills
- how often partners can stay over
- who cleans what and when.

Lodgers in your home

Living with others in a flatshare can be fairly straightforward in many ways as everyone has pretty much equal rights to everything. With lodgers though the situation is different, as one of you owns the property, was there first and will be there after the lodger has gone.

As the situation is ultimately in the hands of the live-in landlord they should be prepared and have thought a few things through prior to the lodger moving in, so you can have a few ground rules and both know where you stand.

One of the first things to decide if you're taking in a lodger is how much of the property they can use. Obviously you'll have your own bedrooms but you need to be clear if there are any areas of the house or flat that are off limits. Your lodger will want to use the kitchen and living room and you can't realistically expect them to spend all their time in their own room. If you've got two bathrooms then that will make life easier but if not then that will be shared space too.

A few points to consider before your lodger moves in are:

THE OTHER HALF

Does your lodger have a partner and, if so, will they expect them to be allowed to stay over? If this isn't okay with you make sure they know this in advance of moving in. You might decide it's fine but set a limit on how many nights a week this can happen, which is also okay as long as you're clear from the outset.

KITCHEN

Clear some space in your cupboards and fridge so your lodger has space for their food.

BATHROOM

What time do you both need to get out of the house by? If you can sort out a routine it'll make things easier in the mornings for both of you.

TV

Just because it's your house doesn't mean you get to decide everything. By taking someone's money for your room you should expect to let them live comfortably in your property. Obviously if you don't ever watch the same programmes this may become tricky but have a look at some of the advice on taking in a lodger in Chapter 4, a little time choosing the right person will make everything easier.

What to do if you can't resolve the conflict

This is the tricky bit as, once communication has broken down completely, there may be no way back. There aren't any quick fixes for situations like this and, sometimes, you'll just have to accept that you don't get on and one (or both) of you would be happier living somewhere else. Obviously if you're a landlord living with a lodger then it's clear which of you will end up moving out.

If there's a conflict between sharers then your landlord may be able to help, depending on what the issue is. You can involve the police or your local council but only in serious conflicts (for example if one of the housemates is threatening or violent).

A voice of experience

Melanie Hill took part in the very first series of *Big Brother* in the UK. We asked her if her time in the house had taught her anything about how to live in a large group:

'Nothing can compare to living under the constant gaze of the *Big Brother* cameras with total strangers. It is a little bit like living in an open prison (or so I would imagine). There's nothing real about living in the *Big Brother* house, it's all contrived and artificial. The most valuable lesson I learnt in the house was tolerance and adapting to change. Every day is totally different with different people coming and going and tasks. My advice to people living with others is try to be a relaxed, calm influence – most things we get stressed about don't really matter in the grand scheme of things so why worry?'

Melanie Hill

CHAPTER SEVEN
Finance and Bills

Money can be one of the most likely causes of arguments amongst flatmates – over 50% of those we surveyed had argued with their flatmates about bills at some point. Arguments over who bought or paid for what, and who actually used it, can lead to all kinds of tension and conflict. The more you plan in advance and sort out your financial arrangements, the more of this you can avoid on a daily basis, leaving you plenty of free time to argue about more important things like football, politics, which pub to go to, why (insert band of choice) aren't as good as everyone says they are, why you don't like Bob's new girlfriend – the list is endless.

Even if you're all clear and organized about the financial side of things, it'll help to read through this chapter and make sure there aren't any unexpected bills you hadn't considered.

Rent

By far the biggest chunk of your money will be going on rent so this is the first thing to sort out. The type of flatshare you live in will determine who you have to pay, it's likely to be one of the following:

- a live-out landlord or agent
- a live-in landlord if you're a lodger
- another housemate who you sublet from.

Whoever you pay it's always a good idea to set up a standing order for your rent so you can make sure it's always paid on time and you don't have to think about it every month. This can be especially important if you live with your landlord as it can put a strain on your relationship if they need to keep asking for money. If you get paid at a certain time of the month it's worth asking if you can pay the rent then as it'll leave you with a clearer idea of how much you've got left for everything else. If not then make sure you don't spend all your money before the rent is due.

If you're renting from a landlord or agent and you all pay the same amount direct to the landlord then things are usually pretty straightforward. If you're renting a whole property and dividing the rent between you things can get a little more complicated – make sure you're clear from the outset who's paying what. It can work well to divide the rent according to who has which room – for example, if there's a big master bedroom with an en-suite then one of you may be happy to pay a bit extra to get that room while whoever has the smallest room pays less. This can also be a great way for a group of people with different income levels to share (and paying the same rent for a single room as someone else does for a double can cause resentment long term). If you're happy to pay different amounts then it would be a good idea to work out who can afford what before you look for a property, as your combined budgets might mean you can afford somewhere better than you previously thought.

If there are particularly desirable rooms then you'll need to work out who gets which. You can make this fun.

Matt says:

'I moved into a flat in North London with a good friend back in the 1990s. The first bedroom was a really big double and either of us would have been happy with it in any other property. Then we saw the loft room, which was huge, and we both wanted it. As neither of us could afford to pay extra to get it we had to find a fair way of deciding.

Tossing a coin is a bit boring so we had a couple of pints and went and played air hockey for the room, figuring there's no skill involved (especially after a couple of pints) so neither of us would have an unfair advantage. The point of air hockey seems to be to hit the thing as hard as you possibly can – if you can break all your opponent's fingers in the process then even better. No fingers got broken but I won and got the room, much to the annoyance of my flatmate's girlfriend (sorry Imogen, have you forgiven me yet?).'

You should check your contract if you're renting a whole property, if you have a 'joint and several' agreement (see Chapter 8, *Contracts, Rights* and *Agreements*) you might find you're all liable if one of you doesn't pay their share. This is fairly standard practice with assured shorthold tenancy agreements as it protects the landlord if one of you fails to pay. It helps to be aware of it from the outset though so you know what you're dealing with if, for example, one of you wants to move out before the agreement is due to end.

Deposits

Under most rental agreements you'll need to pay a deposit before you move in. The standard amount is generally one month's rent (although six weeks is becoming common as well) so you'll have to pay at least two month's rent before you can move in.

The purpose of the deposit is to give the landlord a safeguard against any unpaid rent or damages to the property and furnishings so, provided everything is okay at the end of the tenancy, you should get the full deposit back when you move out. The annoying part is waiting as this usually means, when you next move, you'll need to find another deposit before you get the old one back.

TENANCY DEPOSIT SCHEME

In 2006, the government introduced a new Tenancy Deposit Scheme that requires landlords to hand over your deposit to one of two schemes for safekeeping. This was a result of problems encountered by tenants getting their deposits back – in a recent SpareRoom poll we discovered 65% of people had experienced difficulty getting their deposit back at some point.

For information on deposits and the Tenancy Deposit Scheme, see Chapter 8, *Contracts, Rights and Agreements*.

Bills

Sorting out bills in a shared property can be a nightmare – getting everyone to pay up in full and on time can be a tricky business. Having money conversations with people you're close to can make things awkward, especially if one of you is a little lazy (to put it nicely) when it comes to paying up. However, paying your bills promptly means you won't get faced with a court summons or having your supply cut off, so you might as well get organized.

Some bills, such as council tax, will be easier to deal with, as they're for a fixed amount each month and you can budget accordingly. Others (like gas and electricity) are a little harder as they change each time so become slightly more difficult to budget for.

The bills will all need to be put in someone's name so, unless you live with your landlord and everything's in his or her name, you'll need to sort this out when you move in. It's also vital to check which bills are and aren't included in the rent – water rates and council tax are sometimes paid by the landlord and some rooms are offered all inclusive, so make sure you check what you'll need to pay for on top of your rent before you sign anything.

Remember, having the bills in your name will usually make you liable for any that are unpaid, so don't just put everything in your name to make things easier to sort out.

GAS AND ELECTRICITY

These bills can be the most difficult to deal with as they will be for a different amount each time you pay (especially the bill for whichever heating method you use over the winter months). The fewer of you there are to divide your bills between the quicker (in theory) you should be able to sort them out. Often one person will agree to pay the bill and let everyone else pay them back, which is fine, but this can leave someone seriously out of pocket if the others don't pay up quickly – be warned.

Check with your provider to see if they have any kind of payment plan to help you budget and spread the cost of your bills. At the very least you should contact the supplier with a meter reading when you move in and out and let them know in whose name you want the bill.

'I lived in a shared flat for a year with my girlfriend and a friend of hers. We paid all the bills for gas while we were there (the gas was in my name) but, over a year after we'd moved out, I started getting threatening letters from a debt collection agency saying I owed £850 for gas. Unless we were running a bakery or a hot air balloon business, I can't imagine how they thought three of us could have used this much in a year anyway! I entered into a long correspondence with our gas suppliers (who were extremely unhelpful) but, after almost two years, they eventually stopped pursuing me for the money (especially after I provided a previous tenancy agreement to show I wasn't even living there for part of the period they were trying to make me pay for).'

Steve

KEY METERS

It's common in rental properties, especially shared ones, to have key meters for gas and electricity. These work on a pay-as-you-go basis so you take the key to the nearest top-up point (usually local shops and petrol stations) and put the amount you choose onto it. Once this is getting low you can top-up again. The benefit to the landlord is that the tenants can't run up a huge bill then leave without paying. For tenants it allows them to monitor how much they're spending without getting hit by a huge bill they can't afford. The downside is that most of the gas and electricity suppliers have higher prices for meter customers (and, unless you're really organized, your electricity will run out at a really inconvenient point at least once).

Matt says :
'My first shared flat in London had an electricity key meter and the nearest place you could top it up was a 15-minute walk away. We took it in turns to pay and get top ups but one of us never quite got round to it, so the rest of us ended up paying or having to go out at night to get more put on the key when the power went out. Frustrating is not the word (well, it is but there's a better word which politeness – and my publisher – prevents me from committing to paper).'

PHONE/BROADBAND

The mobile phone is the saviour of flatshares – gone are the days of waiting for three hours to phone out for a takeaway while your flatmate hogged the phone to talk to her boyfriend. Mobiles also mean no boring evenings with a highlighter and the phone bill working out who called which numbers and arguing over the unclaimed ones. You might still need to pay for a landline to get access to broadband but, as long as you don't use it to make calls, that's an easy one to divide between you.

If you, or one of your flatmates, have family overseas who you call on a regular basis you should investigate access numbers. Several companies run these schemes, basically you call them and they put the call through at a much lower cost that most UK phone companies. Just Google 'access number' and the country you need to call.

If you've got broadband it's a great idea to get a wireless router so you can access it from your own computers and rooms. They're not expensive, especially between a few of you, and make it easy for everyone to get online when they need to. Some broadband companies even supply a router when you sign up to their service.

You'll also need to have a conversation at some point about paying for non-essentials like broadband (and cable TV) as some people won't want to pay for services they don't use or want. If some of you want Sky TV, for example, and the others don't then you might find some bills being split between fewer of you. How you deal with this when the people who didn't want it in the first place start watching it is up to you!

COUNCIL TAX

Council tax will be the biggest bill you have to pay and how it gets paid will depend on your situation. Usually one person (known as the 'liable person' for obvious reasons) is liable to pay council tax. This essentially means that the bill is in that person's name, not that it's their responsibility to pay the full amount. Different types of share will mean different ways of paying – here are a few of the most likely scenarios:

Shared house rented by the room

Usually the liable person is whoever lives in the property. If, however, the property is rented by several individuals (or groups) who pay rent separately, the landlord should be the liable person. This will mean the council tax bill is in your landlord's name and he or she will pay. You will possibly still need to pay council tax in this instance but it will most likely be included in your rent.

Shared house rented as a whole

If you rent a whole property, with one contract between you, it's likely you'll have to be responsible for the council tax. This can mean one person has to have the bill in their name, which can lead to problems if one or more people don't pay up. Ask your local authority if it's okay to put the bill in everyone's name as this is fairest and also gives you an extra record of everyone having lived in the property, which can be useful.

You should be able to pay in instalments over the year (or, more commonly, over ten months with a two month break at the end of the financial year), although this might not be possible if you move in the middle of the financial year or fall behind with your payments.

It's essential to inform the council when you move in and out so you don't get stung for a council tax bill for any periods before or after you actually lived in the property.

Lodgers

If you take in a lodger and have previously lived on your own then you'll lose the 25% single occupant discount you've had so far (unless your lodger is a student, in which case you should still be okay). It's reasonable to charge your lodger for his or her half of the council tax (or the increased amount you'll have to pay if you prefer) – this can be included in the rent rather than taking the form of a separate payment. If you're doing this make sure you inform any prospective lodgers that the rent includes council tax.

Students

If some or all of your party are students this will affect your council tax. A flatshare with only students in it is usually exempt from paying council tax. However, if there is a mix of students and professionals then those in employment will still get a council tax bill. As council tax is per household, not per person, the full amount will still be payable (unless there's just one employed person, in which case they can probably apply for a 25% discount). This can mean that some households end up with a couple of people paying a lot of council tax so you should take this into consideration before moving into a mixed house.

An example:

John, Paul, George and Ringo rent a flat for which the council tax bill is £800 a year.

Scenario A

John is at art school full time and Paul is doing a full-time degree in Astrophysics (or something equally rock 'n' roll). George and Ringo both work full time. As John and Paul are both students, and therefore exempt from paying council tax, this leaves the others paying £400 each a year (unless, in the spirit of friendship, they decide to split it four ways anyway).

Scenario B

John and Paul live with other students so their house isn't subject to council tax.

Scenario C

George and Ringo live with two other employed friends (Mick and Keith). Therefore the £800 bill is split four ways and they only pay £200 each.

As you can see, scenario A (where students and those in employment share) results in *someone* paying over the odds – either the students who shouldn't pay at all or the employed sharers who have to take up the shortfall.

Clearly this is a simplified example but you get the picture. We're not saying don't live in a mixed household – just beware of the implications.

WATER

Water bills are another easy one to deal with as suppliers usually bill you for a fixed annual amount and you can spread the payments over at least two terms. However, an increasing number of properties have water meters installed, meaning you pay per usage, so double check first. Some accommodation has the water rates included in the rent so check whether or not this is the case before you move in.

Many people moving out of home for the first time are shocked to get a water bill as they presume water is free – it's not, now you know.

INSURANCE

Your landlord will (or certainly should have) buildings insurance to cover the property but it's a good idea to get your own contents insurance so all your stuff is covered. There are a couple of options for this:

A single contents policy for the flat

Basically you take out insurance to cover the total cost of all your stuff and split the cost between you. This can work out cheaper but you'll need to update the details if one of you moves out and someone else moves in. It can also be tricky working out who needs what coverage (and even if everyone's prepared to pay).

Individual room contents policies

Companies such as Endsleigh offer room contents policies so each of you can insure your own belongings to whatever value you need. This makes it simple for you to protect your own possessions without worrying about everyone else and whether they want to bother with insurance or not. You can then take your policy with you when you move (as long as you let your provider know about your change of address). It's worth checking whether your possessions are covered outside the house as expensive (and easily nickable) stuff like laptops and iPods are going to be taken with you wherever you go. Remember, you're not just insuring against theft, if there was a fire you'd need to replace everything (including your clothes) so take out a policy for a reasonable amount.

Adding your cover to the landlord's insurance

If you live with your landlord they will already have contents insurance and may be happy to add your name to the policy (in return for whatever amount the premium increases by). It may still be easier for you to take out your own room contents policy though, as this will also mean you can take the policy with you when you move and simply update the details with your insurer.

If your landlord says they're going to add you to their policy make sure they actually do as one sharer found out, her's hadn't.

'I lived with my boyfriend and a friend of mine in a two-bed flat for a year or so. We rented the flat from her brother and, when we moved in, he said we could pay him and he'd add us to the existing contents policy (as most of the furniture was his anyway and he had it insured).

We did get burgled while we were there so I was glad we'd paid for insurance but (as it turned out) the brother had taken our money but not actually added our names to the insurance! This made the whole claiming process much trickier as he had to claim for his stuff then give us money towards what we'd lost. Needless to say, we never really got enough to replace everything and we didn't trust our landlord after that.'

Bev

For more information on insurance, including links to companies who offer room contents policies, see: www.SpareRoom.co.uk/essentialguide/insurance.

TV LICENCE

You will need one of these so just cough up and get it over with. It's not so easy to get away without paying these days as the systems used by the licensing people have got more advanced (it's true, I bought a hard disk recorder recently and got a letter from the licensing people saying 'We understand you recently purchased a TV recording device, do you have a licence?' despite the fact that our house already has a licence in my wife's name – Matt).

If it's too much to pay all in one go you can divide the cost over a year. See: www.tvlicensing.co.uk for ways to pay.

Food and shopping

Food is one regular bill that will be difficult to split fairly as everyone eats different amounts and has different tastes. It's worth taking a little time to think about what you buy and use regularly though. Unless you're a really close group of friends and tend to cook and eat together, you probably won't want to buy all your stuff jointly, but it does make sense to have a kitty for some things. After all, there's nothing quite so depressing as five different tubs of butter in the fridge with five different names scrawled on in marker pen – let's face it, everyone will use everyone else's when theirs runs out anyway.

Items like milk, bread, bin bags, butter, toilet roll, cleaning supplies and so on can easily be bought jointly and shared then you can buy other things you want as and when.

A recent poll on SpareRoom showed that around half UK flatshares buy some of their shopping together while the other half just buy for themselves:

- We buy everything together and split the cost – 9%.
- We all buy our own food individually – 52%.
- We buy some stuff together but mostly buy our own – 39%.

Strategy

The first thing to do when you move in is put all the bills in your name and inform the council you're living there so they can sort out your council tax. It's definitely best to put the council tax in everyone's name if you can but bills like electricity you may not want to divvy up, especially if there are several of you in the property.

Next, you need to decide how you're going to pay – it can be easier if one of you pays and everyone settles up with them. If you're going down the 'one person pays the bill' route you should consider each taking responsibility for a bill (i.e. one of you has the electricity in their name and pays that, one does water, one does gas etc.). This will spread the load a bit and make sure no one ends up at their overdraft limit until everyone settles up.

There is the option of everyone just writing a cheque for their share of each bill as it comes in and posting them all together but, as it's generally easier to pay bills online these days, that might be too much hassle. Whoever is responsible for the bills needs to be prompt in paying them, all too often in a flatshare you'll find your supply cut off or get a summons for a bill everyone presumed someone else had paid.

There's a great online resource, which can help you sort out your bills (and general finances) in a shared house, you can find it at: www.ioweyou.co.uk.

Getting behind with your bills

If you do find you get behind with your rent or bills, for whatever reason, there may be something you can do about it, so don't just stick your head in the sand and ignore the problem. What you can do will depend on the nature of the bill and who you're dealing with.

RENT

This is one you'll have real problems with if you fall behind. Don't forget, in most cases, your landlord will need the rent to pay his or her mortgage so if you fall behind it puts them in difficulty too. If you regularly pay late or miss payments you could also be giving your landlord grounds for eviction (see Chapter 8, *Contracts, Rights and Agreements*).

If you think you'll be late paying your rent (whether it's your fault or not) you should give your landlord as much warning as possible. They may not be happy about it but are far more likely to understand if you talk to them than if you just don't pay.

COUNCIL TAX

Getting into arrears with your council tax will eventually lead to a court summons so don't ignore the letters when they start arriving. Also, if you pay monthly and get behind, you may lose the ability to pay in instalments and the council may demand the full amount owing for the rest of the year in one go.

If this does happen it's still worth phoning the council tax office, as they will split the payments if they can – they'd rather you paid than have to take you to court.

UTILITIES

Again with utility bills you will get hounded until you pay up (see Steve's story on page 112) so, if you're struggling, call your supplier and see if they can help work out a payment plan for you. They may also have a scheme to help you spread the cost over a wider period to make things easier.

OTHER BILLS

How other companies treat you when you fail to pay will vary for individual cases. Whoever you're dealing with, a phone call to try and resolve the problem will go down better than no action whatsoever.

With all bill disputes or difficulties, it's important to keep a record of any calls you make (with the name of who you spoke to and the date) and copies of all letters or emails you send and receive. This gives you a record of what has been said in case things escalate and you find yourself in trouble down the line.

IF IT COMES TO THE WORST . . .

If you find yourself with mounting debts you can't pay, you should get in touch with one of the non-profit debt counselling services and get some advice. Financial problems never sort themselves out on their own, once the water starts rising it generally doesn't stop. So, get on the phone and spend £1 on the call rather than buying a lottery ticket (your odds of winning the lottery are 14 million-to-1 yet we still go on hoping – if someone told you there was a 1-in-14 million chance of you being hit by a bus you'd presume it would never happen. Aren't we all optimists at heart! – Matt).

Try:

Consumer Credit Counselling Service
Website: www.cccs.co.uk

National Debtline
Tel: 0808 808 4000

Citizens Advice Bureau
Website: www.adviceguide.org.uk

CHAPTER EIGHT

Contracts, Rights and Agreements

Wherever and however you decide to live, you'll probably find you need to sign an agreement or contract of some kind when you move in. You may think these are in place simply for the benefit of the landlord but, in almost all cases, they protect your rights too so it's useful to know a little about the different types of agreement and what they mean.

The information in this chapter refers mainly to English housing laws; if you live in Wales, Scotland or Northern Ireland, you should check to see if there are any differences in your region. The best source of information of this type is Shelter's website. See the list of useful links at the back of this book, or go to: www.SpareRoom.co.uk/essentialguide/agreements: for links to the relevant pages.

Sharers

If you share a property with several people and pay rent to a landlord, you'll probably fall into one of the following groups:

WHOLE PROPERTY

If you rent the whole property you'll most likely have one contract with all your names on it. If you rent direct from the landlord then he or she will deal with all of this but often the landlord uses a letting agent to find tenants – in this case your dealings will be with the agent. You should be aware that, although the landlord pays the agent, you might have extra costs to pay in this situation.

Additional costs you may encounter include:

Administration fee
This is a one-off payment to cover the cost of drawing-up the contracts.

Reference/credit checking fees
These fees are charged to cover the cost of checking with your bank and employer that you can cover the rent, or checking your credit rating.

Re-signing fee
If you decide to extend your lease at the end of a term, you may be asked to pay a re-signing fee, ostensibly to cover the admin costs of renewing the contracts.

From the perspective of the renter it's hard to see why you should be paying all of these, as the agent is already charging the landlord for their services and is working on his behalf, not yours. These types of fees are

---

Matt says:

'When you sign your contract make sure you've got your landlord or agent's contact details. You may not need them but it's better to double check now than to need something in an emergency (like your boiler breaking down in December) and not be able to get hold of anyone.

Find out who your main point of contact is

This could be your landlord, your agent or whoever manages the property. Ask when you sign the contract who you should call first if there's a problem.

Get a telephone number, preferably a mobile

Make sure you know how to get hold of the person you need. If it's an agent you'll need an out-of-office hours number as well as the regular number.

Ask who you should contact in case of emergency if your landlord or agent isn't available

Get a set of backup contact details in case the first point of contact isn't available. Keep these contact details somewhere you can get at them easily (stuck to the door of the fridge, for example) as you won't want to be emptying out drawers in an emergency.'

---

fairly standard though and there's not much you can do so you'll just have to pay them. One option is to search for lettings that don't use agents or try one of the whole property sites such as: www.findaflat. com. You should always ask beforehand if there will be any additional charges before you sign anything.

Type of contract

You should check to see which type of contract you're signing. By far the most common for rentals in the UK is the assured shorthold tenancy (AST). These are popular as they commit to a fixed term of at least six months and give the landlord more rights and options when it comes to ending a tenancy than an assured tenancy (which gives you the right to remain in a property unless the landlord can convince the court there are good reasons to evict you, such as rent arrears or damage).

The good news about an AST is that it requires the landlord to use a Tenancy Deposit Scheme; at the time of writing, assured shorthold is the only tenancy that requires this. For more on this, see 'Deposits and schemes' later in the chapter.

If you have an AST and the fixed term expires while you continue to live in the property the landlord must get you to sign another fixed term contract or the agreement becomes 'periodic'. Periodic tenancies have different rules and, if you signed for a fixed term, you'll almost always be asked to sign another contract if you remain in the property.

If your contract is joint and several, then this has additional implications, see the boxed text on page 126 for more information on this.

If you have a whole property agreement you should check in advance what the situation is if someone moves out before the agreement expires. The questions you need to ask are:

- If someone moves out, will the rest of us have to pay their rent?
- Can one of us leave before the end of the term if we find a replacement?
- If so, can we change the name on the contract to reflect the new flatmate?
- Will we be charged for this?

Individual contracts

If you rent by the room and each have a separate contract with your landlord then things are a little easier, as each of you is responsible for your own rent and there are no grey areas. You should still check whether you're going to have to pay any additional fees other than a deposit and the first month's rent in advance.

Inter-sharer agreements

One type of agreement which is less common but can prove extremely useful (especially if you rent a whole property) is the inter-sharer agreement. This is a basic contract between flatmates and is separate from any contracts you have with your landlord or agent. The agreement will set out the basic terms under which you share and (crucially) can commit to paper each of your individual obligations regarding rent and bills.

No agreement

If you have moved into an existing flatshare (probably to replace a flatmate who has left) and haven't signed an agreement of any kind then your rights will be limited. In this case your landlord is technically whoever is named in the contract and you're subletting from them. Their contract may well forbid them from subletting in this fashion, which can lead to all sorts of complications. We'd generally advise you to avoid these situations – for more on subletting and other types of tenancy, see Chapter 1.

A note on joint and several contracts

One thing you'll need to check is whether the agreement you have is joint and several – if so, it could mean that the rest of you are liable for any unpaid rent or bills left by any of the other people in the property.

Joint and several is basically a hybrid of joint liability (where all parties are jointly liable for the full amount – in this case rent and bills) and several liability (where parties are liable only for their individual share of the amount).

For an agreement to be joint and several, it must be signed by all parties (council tax is the only exception to this rule). What this type of contract does is allow the claimant (in this case the landlord) to pursue any one party (or tenant) for the full amount owing, it's then up to that tenant to recover what everyone else owes them.

An example

John, Paul, George and Ringo decide to share a flat. They find a great one with four good-sized bedrooms for £500 a month so they sign the agreement and decide between themselves to pay £125 each. After a while the others get fed up with John's new girlfriend, Yoko, hanging round all the time and John leaves to move in with her, naturally he stops paying rent. This leaves Paul, George and Ringo to cover John's share of the rent between them. The landlord won't care that they've agreed between themselves to pay £125 each, he just wants the full rent. He can, if necessary, sue any one of them (not just John) for John's share of the rent if they don't pay up.

   If the boys were students it wouldn't be uncommon for their parents to have signed as guarantors for the rent. Under a joint and several agreement, the landlord could have pursued any one of their parents for the whole amount in the event of any unpaid rent.

Lodgers

If you live as a lodger then things are slightly different. The law recognizes that live-in landlords are more vulnerable if the landlord/ tenant relationship breaks down as they live with their tenant. As a result, live-in landlords aren't required to give as much notice if they want to evict you.

Not all live-in landlords will ask you to sign a contract or pay a deposit but, as more and more people take in lodgers, it's becoming more standard. Your contract should cover, at the minimum:

- how much rent you will pay
- how long the let is for
- what (both of) you need to do if you want to end the agreement prematurely.

It should also cover your deposit if you've paid one.

If you're taking in a lodger, you should also read Chapter 4.

Deposits and Tenancy Deposit Schemes

DEPOSITS
Most landlords will ask you for a deposit when you move into a property. The standard amount is one month's rent (meaning you will have to pay two months up front before you move in), although six weeks isn't uncommon.

The point of a deposit is to protect the landlord against unpaid rent or damages (other than acceptable wear and tear) caused by you. In theory this should mean that, unless you're behind on rent or have damaged anything, you should get your full deposit back promptly after you move out. It doesn't always work this way in practice and, even if you get your deposit back quickly, you'll probably still need to pay a deposit on your next place before you get it back.

Problems with deposits
We asked SpareRoom users if they'd ever had a problem getting their deposit back from a landlord – 65% said they had. The occasional dodgy landlord will try and get a bit of extra cash out of you by claiming they need some (or all) of your deposit for repairs resulting from damages you've caused. Luckily these landlords are few and far between and the new Tenancy Deposit Scheme (see next page) has made a big difference.

Disputes do occur though when a landlord genuinely feels you've damaged either the property or contents and wants to use your deposit to pay for repairs (as he's fully entitled to do if this is the case – that's what the deposit's for after all). That's where the inventory comes into play, see below for information on inventories.

A NOTE ON CLEANING

Most tenancies will require you to leave the property in a fit state to move into for the next tenants, this means cleaning it. If you're expected to clean before you move out, then the property should have been clean for you to move into. If the place is a mess and needs cleaning before you can even move in, you should tell your landlord or agent – it may be the case that you just want to get on and clean it yourself so you can sort your things out but you should still point out that you had to do this.

Check your contract to see what it says about leaving the property clean when you move out. If you don't, then the landlord may be able to keep some of your deposit towards having the property cleaned. Allow time for this when you're packing up and getting out. If you have a day or two crossover period between moving and needing to be out of your old room, then it'll be much easier to clean once all your stuff has gone.

TENANCY DEPOSIT SCHEMES

Since 6 April 2007, all deposits taken by landlords in England and Wales must be protected by a tenancy deposit scheme. The scheme applies to assured shorthold tenancies, the most common type of tenancy agreement. There are two main reasons for this:

• To ensure that when a tenant has paid a deposit and is entitled to get it back that this actually happens;
• To assist in resolving disputes which arise regarding refund of deposits.

The scheme also hopes to encourage landlords and tenants to make clear from the outset the terms and conditions of the lease to avoid disputes occurring.

There are two types of scheme on offer and it is up to the landlord to choose which they will use.

Custodial

- The tenant pays the deposit direct to the landlord who then pays it into the scheme.
- The landlord must provide information to the tenant about the tenancy and which scheme has been used within 14 days.
- At the end of the tenancy, if both parties agree to the amount of deposit returnable, the scheme is notified and returns the deposit as agreed.
- If there is a dispute as to the amount of deposit to be returned, the scheme will hold on to the deposit until the dispute is resolved.
- Interest on payments held during dispute settlement will be used to pay for the running of the scheme with any left over paid to the tenant (or the landlord if the tenant isn't entitled to it).

Insurance-based

- The tenant pays the deposit direct to the landlord.
- The landlord retains the deposit and pays a premium to the insurer.
- The landlord must provide information to the tenant about the tenancy and which scheme has been used within 14 days.
- At the end of the tenancy, if both parties agree to the amount of deposit returnable, the landlord returns the appropriate amount of the deposit.
- If there is a dispute the landlord must hand over the disputed amount to the scheme for safe-keeping until the dispute is settled.
- If the landlord fails to comply, the insurance arrangements will ensure that the tenant receives their deposit back if they are entitled.

Under both schemes, the deposit must be returned within ten days of agreement or settlement of any dispute.

Inventories

If you rent a furnished flat, house or room you will almost always be asked to sign an inventory. An inventory is a list of everything your landlord has provided including furniture, curtains, carpets, kitchenware and appliances. It should also contain information on the condition these items are in at the start of the tenancy (especially noting anything that's damaged). The reason for this is that it makes it much easier to settle disputes about damaged or broken items when you move out if you have an agreed upon list to refer to. This should, in theory, make it easier to get your full deposit back when you move out.

If you're given an inventory to check then don't just treat it as another piece of paper, check it thoroughly. If anything is on the list but you can't find it then make a note. Also note down anything that's damaged if it's not mentioned already. This might all seem like a hassle but it won't take long (especially if you break it up by doing a room or two each) and may well end up saving your deposit further down the line. Give a list of any discrepancies to your agent or landlord.

If your landlord doesn't give you an inventory to check, it would be worth having a quick look round anyway and seeing if anything in the property is broken or damaged. If it is, take a photo of the damage (if you use your phone or digital camera to do this it will probably record the date you took the photo which is a bonus) just in case there's a dispute when you move out.

It's also a good idea to keep any receipts for items you've replaced yourself whilst in the property.

HMOs

'HMO' is the new buzzword in landlord circles and can be a confusing topic as there are plenty of rules and regulations regarding HMOs.

HMO stands for House in Multiple Occupation and is basically a term used to describe certain types of rented accommodation shared by more than one household (meaning the rules don't apply to a house shared by a single family).

If your room is in an HMO, you're probably in one of the following:

• bedsits

- a flatshare where everyone has their own tenancy agreement
- student accommodation (unless you're in halls of residence or other university owned property).

If a property is classed as an HMO, then the landlord has a certain set of obligations towards you, including ensuring:

- proper fire safety measures are in place
- the property isn't overcrowded
- cooking and washing facilities are adequate
- communal areas and facilities are in good repair.

To find out whether you live in an HMO, you can contact a local advice centre by using the Shelter tool located at: http://england.shelter.org.uk/get_advice/advice_services_directory.

Your rights

EVICTION

With the best will in the world, some tenancies run into difficulties. In many cases these can be resolved amicably but, sometimes, this just isn't possible. If your landlord decides to evict you (or if you have a lodger and want to evict them) what can you do?

As a sharer

Your rights will depend on the type of agreement you have. There are laws to protect you in this situation and if your landlord fails to comply with the correct procedures it can be a criminal offence.

Your landlord's reason for wanting to evict you may be based on something you've done or could be due to external factors. The most likely reasons your landlord will want to evict you due to something you've done are:

- failure to pay the rent
- anti-social behaviour
- damaging the property.

In any of these cases there may be something you can do to remedy the situation. If you're behind with the rent this will involve paying any arrears (or convincing your landlord that you can do so).

There may be other reasons your landlord wants you out, such as:

- the property is being repossessed
- they want to sell the property.

If the property is being repossessed there's very little you can do, but if the landlord wants you out so he or she can sell the property they'll need to follow the correct procedures, as laid out in your contract. The type of your tenancy will affect how easily you can be evicted. If you're not sure what type of tenancy you have, you can go to: www.SpareRoom. co.uk/essentialguide/eviction where you'll find a link to Shelter's Tenancy Checker.

Tenancy types and eviction

Assured shorthold tenancy (AST) – Fixed term

As this is the most common tenancy in the UK, we'll start here. If you have an AST then your contract will probably be for a fixed period. If this is the case your landlord will need a legal reason to evict you before the end of the contract. Reasons can include:

- being behind with the rent or being constantly late paying
- you have broken the terms set out in your tenancy agreement
- allowing the property or furniture to fall into disrepair
- causing nuisance or annoyance to others
- the property is being repossessed by the landlord's mortgage lender.

Your landlord will need to give you notice which must:

- be in writing
- give the grounds for eviction
- tell you how long the notice period is (usually 14 days or two months, depending on the grounds).

After the notice period has expired you must leave the property, if not the landlord can apply for a court order. If your fixed term has expired and you're on a periodic tenancy, your landlord may not need grounds for eviction.

Assured tenancy

Most tenancies in the UK are ASTs so, unless your landlord informed you before you moved in that you had an assured tenancy, chances are that's what you'll have. Assured tenants can only be evicted if the landlord has suitable grounds (which is why most people don't use assured tenancies any more) so, providing you pay your rent on time and don't break any of the conditions of your tenancy, you can stay as long as you like.

If your landlord has grounds for eviction, they'll still need to give you notice as they would with an AST.

As a lodger or live-in landlord

Most tenants are protected by the law and have rights that are determined by their living arrangements and the terms of their contract. They can only be evicted under certain circumstances and there are procedures which must be followed. If you share accommodation with your landlord, your rights are different and less comprehensive. This is because the law allows for the fact that a live-in landlord is more at risk if the relationship with their tenant breaks down, than a landlord who lives elsewhere.

All a live-in landlord has to do in this instance is give their lodger 'reasonable notice'. There are no set rules regarding how long reasonable notice is. If there's a contract or agreement that includes a notice period then that will be the minimum period deemed reasonable. Otherwise the amount of notice will depend on several factors, including:

- how long the lodger has been living in the property
- how good the landlord/lodger relationship has been
- how quickly the landlord needs to rent the room out again.

Once the notice period has expired, the landlord has the right to change the locks or remove your belongings from the property. It's always advisable for the landlord in these situations to get a possession order from the court, as they will have no option other than to grant an order if the notice period has expired.

Either using or threatening physical violence whilst trying to evict a lodger (or any kind of tenant) can be a criminal offence.

Harassment

Harassment can be defined as your landlord doing something to interfere with your ability to enjoy living in your home in peace or intended to get you to leave the property. Some landlords think that, by making things difficult for you, they can get you to leave without having to follow the correct procedures. Harassment, either by your landlord or someone acting on their behalf is, however, a serious criminal offence. Just because your landlord owns the property you live in doesn't give them the right to harass you.

Harassment can take many forms and behaviour you may see as unacceptable may seem perfectly reasonable to your landlord. Indeed, he or she may not even be aware that certain behaviour is either inappropriate or unpleasant.

FORMS OF HARASSMENT

There are many kinds of behaviour that could be construed as harassment. The list below is far from exhaustive but contains some of the more common forms of behaviour encountered by tenants:

Visiting your home too often or without warning

The fact that he or she owns it doesn't give your landlord the right to just turn up whenever they want to see how you're keeping it. Your landlord should give you at least 24 hours' notice before coming to visit the property, and coming round to check up on you too often can be seen, in some cases, as harassment.

It's natural that your landlord will want to check that everything is okay and that you're not mistreating or damaging the property, but occasional visits with plenty of warning should be the rule.

Entering the property when you're not there or without your permission.
Your landlord has no right to keep a key to the property (unless this is stated in the tenancy agreement) and should never enter the property while you're out unless you've given permission. As stated above, if your landlord needs to access the property you should be given plenty of notice and a time should be agreed that's acceptable to you.

Restricting your access to utilities such as gas, water or electricity
Your landlord isn't allowed to interfere with your ability to access utilities supplied to the property in an attempt to get you to move out. This includes non-payment of bills in order to restrict your access.

Allowing the property to deteriorate to the point where it's dangerous
Your landlord has an obligation to maintain the property to a standard fit for you to live in. Failure to do so can be seen as harassment, particularly if done intentionally with the aim of getting you to move out.

Rupert says:
'The first student house I lived in (with Matt, as it happens) had a leaky kitchen ceiling. We reported it to our landlord but nothing happened and, gradually, the problem got worse. Eventually the whole ceiling came down, narrowly missing my friend's head. We no longer had the problem of a leaky ceiling as we didn't have a ceiling. Eventually it got sorted but it took far longer than it should have.'

Sending builders or workmen round without warning
If your landlord needs to do any work to the property (or any of the appliances or furnishings in it) he should contact you first so you know this is happening and, wherever possible, arrange a convenient time for the work to take place. Obviously your landlord will have to work to the availability of whoever is carrying out the repairs so won't necessarily be able to arrange things to suit you but should certainly see if there's a mutually acceptable time for the work to be done.

Stopping you from having guests

As a tenant you have the right to have guests to stay in the property, unless of course your contract forbids or restricts this.

Threatening you

Threatening behaviour towards you by your landlord (or someone acting on their behalf) can be a criminal offence. You have the right to enjoy the property in peace and any attempt to interfere with this can be reasonably seen as harassment.

WHAT SHOULD I DO?

Talk to your landlord

The first thing you should do is talk to your landlord – in some cases he or she may not even realize their behaviour is upsetting or inconveniencing you. Even if you suspect your landlord is harassing you deliberately, it's worth having the conversation as you may at least find out why it's happening.

Keep records

Once you've done this, unless the situation improves, you should keep a record of all incidents in case you need it for reference later on. You should also put all your communication with your landlord in writing and request that they do the same – if you have a conversation follow it up with a letter confirming what was said so you have it in writing as well. It may be a good idea to have someone else with you if you need to see your landlord.

Seek advice

You have several options if you need to take action. The Citizens' Advice Bureau may be able to help – you should certainly have a look at their online advice guide at: www.adviceguide.org.uk. Your local council should also be able to help and you should report any incidents of harassment to them. You should only go to the police to report serious incidents.

Remember, any action you take is likely to have an effect on the relationship you have with your landlord and things may well get unpleasant enough that you want to move out anyway.

Problems getting hold of your landlord

From time to time you'll need to get hold of your landlord. Sometimes it will be with a quick question that can wait a few days, sometimes (for example, if your boiler has packed up and it's the middle of winter) it's more urgent. Your contract should include your landlord's contact details or those of the agent managing the property so double-check that when you sign. Make sure you have an alternative contact person in case you can't get hold of your landlord or agent in an emergency – this is especially important if your landlord lives abroad.

Matt says:

'My current landlord lives in Turkey so my initial point of contact is a friend of his who lives nearby. My boiler broke in the middle of winter last year; without a local contact to sort it all out it would have taken ages to get anything done (and it took long enough as it was).'

If you've tried contacting your landlord and can't get through or get a reply to your messages and your landlord used an agent you can try calling the agent. They may have an alternative number or be prepared to call on your behalf. If you still can't get a response or don't have an agent to try then you should get in touch with the Citizens' Advice Bureau and see what they recommend as a next step.

Shelter's advice directory can help you find someone to talk to if you need help. Or you can go to www.SpareRoom.co.uk/essentialguide/eviction for links to this and other useful resources.

CHAPTER NINE
Flatshare in London

With a population of 7.5 million, and a surrounding commuter belt which doubles that figure, London has by far the most thriving flatshare population in the UK (and one of the busiest in the world). High numbers of students, graduates and young professionals (plus a large transitory population) means the demand for both short- and long-term temporary accommodation is high.

Look at any research into the most expensive cities in the world and London will be right up there (along with Moscow, New York and Tokyo). House prices are high (despite the recent downturn in the property market) and the cost of living is far from cheap, so shared accommodation is the only choice for many Londoners and visitors.

As a result there's always a high demand for rooms over a wide range of budgets and a huge variety of accommodation available. Whether you're looking for a cheap room in a shared house or something in a luxury Chelsea flat with river views there's something out there if you can afford the rent.

A few common questions

ISN'T LONDON HORRENDOUSLY EXPENSIVE?

Compared to most places in the UK (and most places in the world), London is an expensive city to live in. However, rents vary enormously from area to area, so get online and browse a few ads to see what's on offer and get an idea of how much rent you'll need to pay each month.

IS IT SAFE?

The simple answer to this is yes. As with any large city there are certain risks though and there are things you can do to minimize your chances of having anything unpleasant happen to you. See 'Staying safe' on page 149 for more on this.

HOW CAN I FIND ACCOMMODATION?

Online advertising has made it easier than ever to search for a flatshare. If you're coming from outside London, you can do some research into areas, prices and the kind of rooms available long before you get to London. See 'Finding accommodation in London' below for advice on finding somewhere to live.

HOW EASY IS IT TO GET AROUND?

London has a great network of buses, tubes and trains, so wherever you live, it's easy to get to where you want to go. Have a look at 'Getting around' later in the chapter for information on public transport in London.

WHERE SHOULD I LIVE?

There's no easy answer to that I'm afraid – ask half a dozen Londoners and you'll probably get half a dozen answers. Some people swear by North London, some insist South is better and everyone has their favourite places to live. Where you end up will most likely be dictated by your budget and where you need to be for work or study and, once you've been in London for a while, you'll develop your own list of top spots.

'Finding accommodation in London' (below) has some advice to help get you started in your search.

Finding accommodation in London

Finding somewhere to live in London can be a daunting process, especially if you're new to the city. With so many areas to choose from, and so much accommodation on offer, it can be bewildering at first. You'll have a much better chance of narrowing down your search if you answer a couple of basic questions; this will help you discount lots of areas and concentrate your search on the places likely to be best for you.

WHERE DO YOU NEED TO BE?

Whether you're working, studying or just visiting, it makes sense to start looking for accommodation based on where you'll need to be. Living close to where you'll spend most of your time not only cuts down your commute, but will also reduce the amount you spend on travel.

If you already know people in London, you might want to consider living near them. It's certainly worth picking their brains about areas if you can, and going down to stay for a weekend or two before you move, to get a sense of where the different areas are in relation to each other and what they're like.

WHICH AREA?

Popular areas for flatshare in London

Try going to SpareRoom's London homepage (http://london.SpareRoom. co.uk) and have a look at the list of popular London areas on the right hand side. This will give you an idea of the areas that get searched for most on the site – these areas are consistently the most popular and there will always be a good selection of rooms on offer for each.

The list includes:

- Angel
- Brixton
- Balham
- Battersea
- Clapham
- Docklands
- Ealing
- Fulham
- Greenwich
- Hackney
- Hammersmith

- Hoxton
- Islington
- Putney
- Shoreditch
- Wimbledon

Popular commuter areas a little further out include:

- Crawley
- Croydon
- High Wycombe
- Maidenhead
- Slough
- Stevenage
- Windsor

Traditionally, the busiest areas for flatshare in London were South and West of the city, with areas such as Clapham and Ealing topping the lists. Recently though, the Docklands area (and East London in general) has seen a sharp rise in the number of rooms available and people looking to live there. This is mostly due to the relocation of much of London's financial business to Canary Wharf and a huge improvement in transport links to the area. This regeneration of East London was sparked by the Canary Wharf development and continued with the building of the Millennium Dome in Greenwich. With the 2012 Olympic Games set to be held in East London, this regeneration is still very much in evidence and is likely to add to the growing demand for shared accommodation in the area.

Docklands is now regularly the busiest area for flatshare in London, and therefore the UK. The map on page 142 shows which London areas have the most rooms to rent, the darker an area, the more rooms there are on offer. Docklands falls into the borough of Tower Hamlets, which as you can see, is one of the busiest areas.

Fig. 1. London rooms

A FEW POINTERS

There isn't space in this book to go into detail about all the areas of London and what they're like, so we've put together a list of a few popular areas by type, just to give you a starting point for your research.

Trendy

- Shoreditch
- Stoke Newington
- Hoxton
- Crouch End

Busy
- Brixton
- Hackney
- Camberwell
- Shepherd's Bush

Cheap
- Walthamstow
- Lewisham
- Tooting

Well-heeled
- Islington
- Crouch End
- Clapham
- Dulwich

Downright posh
- Hampstead
- Chelsea
- Fulham
- South Kensington

Leafy
- Wimbledon
- Finsbury Park
- Epping
- Richmond

Suburban
- Ealing
- Southgate
- Barking

Villagey
- Highgate
- Hampstead
- Dulwich Village
- Blackheath

Central
- Soho
- Covent Garden
- The City

Riverside
- Richmond
- Kew
- Docklands
- Barnes

Alternative
- Camden

WHAT IF I CAN'T AFFORD IT?
The majority of people moving to London for the first time have unrealistic expectations of what they'll be able to afford. Most people can't stretch to a room right in the middle of town so most of London's flatsharing population lives a little further out. Unsurprisingly, the areas with high house prices are similarly expensive to rent in – areas like Clapham, Islington and Fulham are good examples of this. If you can't

afford the area you really like, a good tip is to look next door or slightly further out.

Maybe you love Clapham but just can't afford the rents – try Tooting, it's a popular area for flatsharing and is on the same tube line as Clapham, so you'll still be able to go out there. Similarly, if Fulham is where you want to be but the budget just won't stretch, have a look just over the river in Putney (which doesn't have quite the swanky image Fulham does, saving you a few pounds a week on rent). Fancy trendy Stoke Newington? Dalston has less of the cool factor and, accordingly, rents are cheaper (plenty of people who live in Dalston claim their flat is in Stoke Newington anyway! – Matt).

One of the joys of London is that there's always something to do and somewhere new to try – just because you can't afford to live somewhere, doesn't mean you can't go out there. As long as you've got a decent pub, restaurant, bar or cinema near enough for a local night out, the rest is easily available by public transport.

GOING OUT OR STAYING IN?

The temptation in London is to want to live in a busy, vibrant area with lots going on. There's nothing wrong with that, plenty of people live in busy areas, but it's worth thinking about how much you'll be taking advantage of them. You can always go out to somewhere busy but you can't make an area quieter than it is if you want a bit of peace. Why not live somewhere within easy reach of the area you love so you can go there when you want to but take advantage of the quiet life (and probably lower rents) a little further out?

WHAT'S YOUR BUDGET?

Once you've worked out which areas in general will be best, you can start looking at how much you can afford to pay. With rooms in London ranging from £350 per month to over £1,000 (with some even higher – SpareRoom recently had a listing for a room in Chelsea for £1,500 a month), there are bound to be areas you just can't afford. Typically, the closer to the centre of town you are, the more you should expect to pay, but things get interesting once you start looking a little further out.

North London is often more expensive than South as there are far more tube stations North of the river (there are more tube stations with access to more than one line North of the river than there are tube stations in total South of the Thames). However, many South London areas have overground train stations that actually get you into the city quicker as they stop less frequently than tubes. Also, West London is traditionally more expensive than East, although the gap is getting smaller as more of East London is redeveloped.

Have a look at the map below; it shows London boroughs by average room rental – the darker areas are more expensive than the lighter ones. Obviously, there will be different areas within each borough with differently priced rooms but this will give you a general idea which areas are likely to be cheapest.

Fig. 2. Map: London rents

How to look

Traditionally, print advertising, in publications such as *Loot*, was the best place to look for accommodation in London. With the advent of online flatshare sites, it's now far easier to use the Internet to find a room. The first London flatshare site (and the first UK site we know of) was: www.IntoLondon.com, founded in 1999. As the site grew and demand rose the site was expanded in 2004 to cover the whole of the UK and SpareRoom was born.

IntoLondon is still one of the leading London-specific sites and is a great place to look for a room. SpareRoom also has a dedicated London section at: http://london.SpareRoom.co.uk.

A COUPLE OF HANDY SEARCH TOOLS

SpareRoom's 'advanced search' function gives you the opportunity to search outwards from the centre of London based on the 'zones' system used to organize public transport in the city (for more on this see 'New to London – Getting Around' later in the chapter). This gives you the ability to search for rooms in specific zones, which can help you target the areas you need to look in.

Another great tool is the 'tube line search'. Once you've found the nearest tube station to your work or study, you can search for properties by the line it's on. You can also search by commute time from or to a specific station. Used in conjunction with the other 'advanced search' functions (such as budget) you can really tailor your search to find the best place. To use this function simply click on 'advanced search' on SpareRoom's homepage.

PLACE A 'ROOM WANTED' AD

You can let people know you're looking for a room by placing a 'room wanted' ad. This allows you to tell prospective flatmates where you're looking, what you're looking for and how much you can afford. Room advertisers search the wanted ads and get email updates so you may just find the perfect flatshare comes looking for you. For advice on placing a wanted ad have a look at Chapter 2, *Find a Flatshare*.

SPEED FLATMATING

Another great way of finding accommodation in the capital is to visit one of the regular Speed Flatmating™ events held in Central London. Speed flatmating is designed to give those looking for a room in London the chance to meet people with rooms available (both people looking for a lodger and sharers replacing a flatmate who's leaving). The best thing about this way of finding somewhere to live is that it lets you meet the people before you see the room. As we all know, an average property with great people is always better than a fantastic one with flatmates you don't get on with.

Speed flatmating is held in a Central London bar and can be a relaxed way to meet a few potential flatmates without having to commit to anything on the spot. It's also a great night if you're new to London as it'll give you the chance to get to know a bit about the accommodation you can expect to find and quiz people about different areas.

Speed Flatmating was the brainchild of SpareRoom's Gemma Allen-Muncey.

Gemma says:

'I first thought of speed flatmating shortly after we launched SpareRoom.co.uk in April 2004. Rupert and I were having a discussion about how we could improve the service we offer our users and whether there was anything else we could offer other than the online advertising. A friend had been to a speed dating event the evening before and as I was telling Rupert about this something clicked and I thought "what about Speed Flatmating events?".

We ran the first event in Clapham Junction in June 2004 and it was a huge success. The really great thing about speed flatmating is that, not only does it enable people to meet with loads of potential flatmates in one evening in a safe environment, it's also really good fun for everyone who attends and we get a lot of people leaving as friends. The events are successful for most who attend and from the very first event we noticed the unexpected outcome of roomseekers buddying up with other roomseekers and forming new houseshares together. We've now modified the event format to take this into account and as a result the events have become even more popular.'

Speed flatmating worked for me

'I found out about speed flatmating while surfing the Internet in a bid to find a room in London. I was curious to see if it would be an easier way to find a room as I was a bit overwhelmed with all the other sites and trying to find time to organize viewings.

I went along to the event, which was held in a bar – this was great as it was on neutral ground rather than someone's house, which can seem a bit like going to a job interview!

I spent a few minutes with about 10 or 11 people with rooms to let and was able to quickly work out which ones I was interested in going to view by asking questions about price, location, local amenities etc. – it certainly saved me a lot of time.

I organized a meeting with my favourite one and loved it immediately, so I can certainly say for me it was a really effective and enjoyable process with a great end result!'

Freya

For more information on speed flatmating, go to: www.speedflatmating. co.uk.

TYPES OF LET IN LONDON

Having the biggest flatshare population in the UK means London also has the widest choice of types of flatshare – if it exists you'll probably find it somewhere in London. Monday to Friday lettings are much more popular in London than most other areas as many people commute long distances to work in the capital and it can be easier to stay during the week and go home for weekends.

The lodger's view

'I have a family home in Norfolk and commute to London during the week, where I rent a room Monday to Friday. It's really a case of what's best for the family vs what's best for income purposes and the benefits and drawbacks are mostly personal rather than financial. If you can find someone who's prepared to rent to you just for weekdays it can work out really well for them as they can earn a little bit of extra income without losing all their privacy.'

Dan

For more information on the different types of let you'll encounter and which will best suit you see Chapter 1, *Types of Let*.

Staying safe

London is a busy 24-hour city and, as in any other city, crime does exist. In general though London is a safe place to live; by using your common sense and observing a few simple precautions (which apply to anywhere, not just London) you can reduce the chances of anything unpleasant happening to you.

DON'T MAKE YOURSELF AN OBVIOUS TARGET

Pickpockets and thieves generally look for easy targets; if you keep a close eye on your belongings and don't draw attention to yourself your chances of having your possessions stolen is much lower.

- Keep an eye on your bag wherever you are and don't leave it open.
- Don't use your mp3 player when walking home alone at night.
- Put your purse or wallet away before you walk away from cash machines.
- Be discrete using your mobile.

DRINK

Booze is a contributing factor in a large percentage of crimes committed. In some respects, however, London feels particularly safe at night. As there are so many reasons for people being out late at night (theatre, restaurants, pubs, cinema, gigs), there's a wide range of people using public transport so getting home can feel less threatening that it does in some smaller towns.

Be careful when you're out on the town not to get so drunk you're not in control. Chances are nothing unpleasant will happen to you but being legless makes you an easy target (especially if you're female), so know your limits.

Keep an eye on your drink when you're in pubs or clubs (or get a friend to), don't leave it unattended and run the risk of having it spiked.

GETTING HOME

If you're out late at night on your own, make sure you know how you're going to get home at the end of an evening and tell someone where you are. Public transport in London is excellent and runs until late so your options for getting home are usually pretty good. If you're going to get a cab home always get a black cab or a mini-cab from a licensed firm or office. Illegal cabs do operate and can be dangerous (for reasons ranging from their being uninsured to attacks on single female passengers). For more information on using public transport, see page 151.

New to London

If you're moving to London for the first time, there are a few things you'll need to know to help you find your way around and get to know the city.

POSTCODES

London is made up of a collection of boroughs but you're more likely to hear people refer to where they live by which tube or train station it's nearest to. Additionally, general areas are often referred to in order to make things easier (e.g. South East, North West, Docklands, and so on). One of the main ways used in flatshare adverts to distinguish areas is the postcode. Now flatshare websites show maps and contain more detailed information on location it's not as essential to know your postcodes as it used to be (in print ads the only indication as to where a property was would be the postcode). It's still handy to understand a little about how postcodes work though.

Most property adverts and estate agents in London (and the rest of the UK) refer at some point to the postcode of the area the property is in, which can be confusing if you're not used to the system. Basically, all London postcodes are made up of two different sections. Take the following as an example:

N11 3RN

The first part refers to the general area the property is in (in this case, New Southgate) and, as a rule, it is this part you will find in property adverts. The second part refers to the street and location of the property on that street. The prefixes of the first part are straightforward (for example SW refers to South West) and give the general part of London, whereas the number gives a more specific location. However, geographically, the numbering appears arbitrary as, for instance, NW1 is central, whereas NW2 is far out and does not border NW1. This is because when the numbered system was first introduced in 1917, the postcodes numbered 1 (E1, NW1, W1, SW1, SE1) were most central and the subsequent numbers assigned alphabetically by the name of the district they represented. The exceptions to this are the central London postcodes of EC and WC (East Central and West Central respectively). See *Appendix – London Postcodes* for a list of London postcodes and areas they cover.

GETTING AROUND

The most useful tool you'll need to navigate your way around London, whether you're on foot, public transport, bike or car, is an A–Z. These handy London street maps come in various sizes (including handy pocket or handbag sized editions), are available at bookshops and newsagents, and will help you work out where you're going until you get used to London.

Matt says:

'I've lived in London for 12 years and still use an A–Z regularly. I've got a little pocket-sized one to carry around and a bigger one with more detail and a wider coverage that I keep at home.'

PUBLIC TRANSPORT

Zones explained

The first thing you'll need to get your head around is the concept of zones. London Transport (LT), the authority who oversee all aspects of travel in the city, have divided London into six zones which start centrally with Zone 1 (covering the City and Westminster) and spread out in concentric circles to cover the rest of London and some areas of the commuter belt which are actually outside Greater London altogether. You can get a free map from LT that shows the layout and coverage of Zones 1–6. This map can be obtained at tube and train stations and is handy to keep in your wallet or handbag for quick reference when you're out and about.

Wherever you live in London you'll need to get around and, despite the tendency of Londoners to complain about public transport whenever the opportunity arises, things aren't as bad as you'll be led to believe. With a large network of tubes, buses and trains to choose from, the capital and surrounding areas are pretty well covered, and the more you travel the better you'll get at working out the easiest and quickest way of getting where you need to be.

For more information about planning your journey, visit: http://journeyplanner.tfl.gov.uk.

Travel cards/Oyster cards

The whole ticketing system on London transport changed with the introduction of Oyster cards. Oyster is a pay as you go ticketing system that operates by means of smart cards. The card is read by a sensor in ticket barriers on tube stations so, providing you 'touch in' and 'touch out' at the beginning and end of your journey, it can work out how far you've travelled and deduct an appropriate amount from your card. The card can be topped up at stations or online and buses, and trams also have card readers installed in them. If you travel several times during a day, the fare is capped at a level which is cheaper than buying a one-day travelcard.

Oyster fares are cheaper than buying standard paper singles, in an attempt to get people to switch over from standard tickets. A cash bus and tram fare costs £2.20, while the single Oyster fare is £1.30, but capped at £4 for any number of trips in a day. On the underground, a single in Zone 1 costs £1.90 with Oyster (£4 paper). At present, most overground train stations are not set up to use pay as you go Oyster so you'll still need to buy a travelcard if you use the rail network regularly.

For information on getting hold of an Oyster card in advance of coming to London, check out TFL's web page: https://oyster.tfl.gov.uk/oyster.

TYPES OF TRANSPORT

Tube

Officially called London Underground, but known to most as 'The Tube', the network of subterranean lines criss-crossing London is world famous. Twelve lines cover the capital from East to West and North to South, and the colour-coded map that represents them is a familiar image to most these days. The lines themselves are referred to by name rather than colour (e.g. Central line, Victoria line etc.), so you need to know the name of the line you want to use. The map is available free from tube stations and is easy enough to follow as lines are listed by both name and colour. Once in a station, the direction for platforms for each line is usually indicated by both name and colour as well, so all you'll need to do is make sure you're on the right platform for the direction you want. Most platforms have a large sign on the opposite wall from the platform (i.e. on the other side of the tracks) that shows the line you're on and indicates which direction trains from that platform are travelling in (including the stations you'll travel through after leaving the station you're at). This gives you plenty of opportunities to double check you're getting on the right train (I still occasionally get on the right tube line but going in the wrong direction if I'm not paying attention – Matt).

Unlike many other underground networks, the Paris Metro for example, the tube lines aren't named by terminus but by direction (eastbound, northbound, westbound or southbound) so, having reached the line you need, check your map to see which direction you need to go in. Be aware that some lines (District and Northern for example) split into different branches outside Central London, so check you're getting on the right train. This may all seem a little complicated at first but you'll get used to it quickly and will soon find you don't need the map for many shorter journeys to familiar stations.

The big advantage of tubes is that they are frequent (more so than trains) and it's easy to see when you need to get off (unlike buses) so you can't really go too far wrong. If you do get a bit confused as to where you're going there are maps on most platforms and often members of London Underground staff (usually dressed in blue) you can ask. Failing that you can always ask a fellow passenger as most Londoners pride themselves on knowing how to get about (just ask a group of people the quickest way to get from Richmond to Chalk Farm and watch the debate unfold). Tubes run from early morning to around midnight on most lines but check when your last train is to be on the safe side.

You'll find a downloadable tube map at: www.intolondon.com/tubemap.

Trains

Whilst tubes are often the best bet for navigating the inner parts of the city, trains are great for the outlying zones and beyond. Firstly, you get daylight and fresh air on trains (a definite bonus in the summer), and secondly, the distance between stations is greater so you'll get further more quickly. Trains aren't as frequent as tubes but often serve areas with no tube connections, particularly south of the Thames. Whilst you're within the six zones of the transport system your travelcard covers you for train travel as well as tubes so if it's easiest to get where you're going by train (or if the tubes aren't working!) then it's not a problem. Bear in mind that Oyster pay as you go doesn't cover most of the rail network yet.

When travelling by train it's handy to know exactly when your trains go as missing one by 30 seconds and having to wait 25 minutes is a real pain, especially if you've forgotten your book! You can get train information by calling: 08457 48 49 50 or online at http://www.thetrainline.com.

Buses

There aren't many better ways to see a city than from the top deck of a bus and London is no exception. Buses are usually slower than tubes but, especially since the introduction of congestion charging (see page 157) on London's streets, things are getting better. Despite the fact that London's buses are owned and operated by a number of different companies, they all operate in the same way and recognize the zonal system and accept travelcards, Oyster and bus passes. Some buses now require you to buy a ticket before boarding; signs at bus stops will tell you which buses this applies to.

The bus network is more complicated than the tube and can take a while longer to work out, but bus stops have maps and boards to show you the routes they serve and the numbers of routes serviced by a particular stop are displayed on the bus stop sign itself. Buses display these numbers both on the front and back and, increasingly, on the side by the front doors. The display on the front will also show the final destination of the bus along with major stops along the way. There is also an extensive network of night buses that travel throughout the night, long after tubes and trains have stopped.

Although the iconic Routemaster double decker buses have been replaced with newer models, including the extra long 'bendy buses' on some routes, they still operate on a couple of heritage routes. These buses have been repainted to look the way they did in the 1960s so a trip on one is a great way to see a bit of London in classic style. The two routes serviced at present are Royal Albert Hall to Aldwych and Trafalgar Square to Tower Hill.

DLR

DLR or Docklands Light Railway was opened in the late 1980s to connect the Docklands area and parts of South-East London to the City. Trains go from Bank and Tower Hill out through Canary Wharf and Greenwich to Lewisham and up to Stratford to link with the Jubilee Line. For some areas the DLR is the easiest option and, now the Jubilee Line covers more of the same areas, is much more integrated with the rest of the transport network. The first time you use it you may feel (especially on some of the elevated sections around Canary Wharf) like you're on a safari park style monorail but that all adds to the fun.

River

As London is on the Thames it's possible to get around by water (as long as the places you need to get from and to are both near the river that is). There are piers all along the river through central London from Putney to Woolwich and regular services run between them. You should be aware though that travelcards aren't valid on river services so you'll have to pay extra to use them. This makes them less than ideal for commuting which is a pity as a journey to work along the river would be a great start to the day (in most weather conditions anyway).

Whether you use the river to get around or not you should definitely take a sightseeing trip along the Thames at some point as it's a great way to see some of the highlights of London's heritage (such as the Houses of Parliament, Tower Bridge, St. Paul's and The Tower of London). For a great way to see the best of London by both road and river (and this has nothing to do with flatshare or London transport so please forgive me), have a look at www.londonducktours.co.uk.

For more info on getting around on the river see: www.tfl.gov.uk/gettingaround/9442.aspx.

Bike

As with many large cities, a bicycle can be a great way to get around. With the congestion charge reducing traffic in the city centre (and increasing the cost of driving) many people have opted to switch to bike. There is an extensive network of cycle routes around London that make it easier to avoid the traffic. For more details check out: http://www.tfl.gov.uk/tfl/roadusers/cycling/maps/maps-and-guides.aspx.

Taxis and cabs

Anyone who's spent time in London will be familiar with the sight of a black cab. Along with the red double decker Routemaster buses they are one of the most iconic images of the London streets. For short journeys in the centre of town and getting home late at night, taxis can be invaluable, just flag one down on the street and away you go.

Minicabs can often be cheaper than taxis, especially on longer journeys, so look out for licensed minicab offices too. Be careful though as there are a large number of unlicensed minicabs operating in London and, apart from being uninsured, these can be highly dangerous. These generally operate by hanging around busy areas and touting for business. Licensed cabs should all have their licence on display so check before you get in. To find a licensed private hire operator, go to: https://www.tfl.gov.uk/tfl/gettingaround/findaride/default.aspx.

You can also text 'home' to 60835 to receive a text message listing local hire firms.

DRIVING

Driving in London has a certain stigma attached to it, especially for those who have never tried. London is one of the busiest cities in the world and, naturally, traffic can be horrendous but don't let that put you off. As long as you're well prepared and able to stay relatively calm you'll be fine. The first and most important thing to know is where you're going and how to get there – if you've done a bit of homework you'll find yourself less likely to be going round in circles for the afternoon. A good street atlas or A–Z is essential – there are so many good ones available that it's probably best to pop into a bookshop and compare a few to see which covers the areas you need and is easiest to read. You can also get detailed routes with instructions to print out from the AA and RAC at: www.theaa.com and www.rac.co.uk.

Other than knowing where you're going, it's also worth knowing a couple of other things, firstly about congestion charging.

Congestion charging

By far the biggest change to driving habits in the capital in recent times has been the introduction of congestion charging. Congestion charging came into effect on 17 February 2003 and was intended not only to decrease traffic on the city's roads but also to encourage people onto (and increase funding for) public transport. The scheme works by charging vehicles to enter Central London. The designated zone inside which the charge applies stretches from Marylebone and Euston Road in the North, and Kensington in the West, to Lambeth and Newington in the South, and Tower Bridge Road and Commercial Street in the East.

There's a free through route which starts at Vauxhall Bridge Road in the South and runs through to Edgware Road but you should expect this to be busy.

The charge applies from 7am to 6pm Monday to Friday (excluding public holidays) and the cost for one day is £10 if you pay before midnight on the day of travel. You can also pay the following day at an increased cost of £12 (this effectively means next charging day so, if you travel on a Friday you have until midnight on the Monday to pay the next day fee). Methods of payment include shops and garages, telephone and online payment and even payment by SMS text message.

There are plenty of warning signs on the roads around the zone plus several on motorways and A roads coming into London, so (in theory) you should be well aware of where the boundaries are. In practice it helps to be aware before you travel if you may need to enter the zone. Several pocket maps are available showing the exact boundaries of the zone (both A–Z and the AA publish maps such as these and they are readily available in petrol stations and bookshops around London) and most A–Zs have it clearly marked. If you're heading into London but won't be entering the congestion charging zone it's also important to bear in mind roads such as the North and South Circular Roads (A406 and A205) are often busier as a result of traffic avoiding Central London.

If you drive a motorbike or scooter, you should be exempt from the charge. Also, anyone driving an electrically powered car is exempt.

For more information on the congestion charge and how to pay, log on to the official website: http://www.tfl.gov.uk/roadusers/congestioncharging/default.aspx.

Parking

After the congestion charge, the second most hotly-debated issue concerning driving in London is parking. Parking in and around London can be difficult and expensive and restrictions apply in the centre of the city from 8.30am to 6.30pm Monday to Friday and 8.30am to 1.30pm on Saturdays. Meters and car parks are expensive and it's not even guaranteed you'll find anywhere to park at all. Further out in the more residential areas, parking conditions vary wildly – in some areas you may even need to buy a permit to park outside your own house.

Useful contacts for parking in central London:

NCP (National Car Parks)
Website: www.ncp.co.uk
Tel: 0870 606 7050

For more information on all aspects of travel in London, go to: http://www.tfl.gov.uk/home.aspx.

CHAPTER TEN

Staying Safe

The Internet has changed our lives in so many ways. We can shop, chat, play games, find information – the benefits are endless. The downside is that the Internet provides the possibility of concealing your identity, making it possible to conduct scams and fraud in new ways.

The aim of this chapter is not to scare you into thinking the Internet is unsafe, but to give you a little information with which to approach any transaction confidently. Roads are dangerous to cross, so rather than tell our children never to cross roads, we give them the knowledge they need to reduce the risks and navigate them safely. Rather than say 'Never cross the road, it's dangerous', we tell them 'Don't cross without an adult' or 'Always use the pedestrian crossings and remember to look both ways'.

Just as you wouldn't cross the road without performing a few simple checks, you shouldn't conduct any form of business online without a similar amount of caution. The following information should give you the guidance you need to 'look both ways' before parting with any money as well as some basic advice to follow, whether you found your room online or not.

Online safety

In any online transaction involving a relatively large amount of money, there will always be risks but, by learning a little about how the scams operate (and using a safe website), you can drastically reduce the chance of anything untoward happening to your or your money.

USE A REPUTABLE SITE

The first thing to do is decide which website(s) you want to use. By picking a reputable site you've taken the first step to avoid scams, as the site should be filtering listings before they even hit your screen. Sites that require users to register before they can respond to listings have the added benefit of another level of safety in place so, although it may seem like a pain to have to register your details, it has its benefits in terms of security.

HOW SITES PROTECT YOU

By providing a space for you to advertise sites should feel an obligation to do their utmost to ensure any fraudulent listings or scam attempts are dealt with. There's plenty a site can do to keep its users safe. As an example here are some of the tactics we employ at SpareRoom to make sure your experience with us is positive.

Man + Machine = Security

SpareRoom has a team of dedicated staff who spend their time checking the listings submitted before they go live. With over a million registered users, it's not possible to check every single ad so that's where the machines come in. We have an extensive (and ever growing) set of filters we run all our listings through which are set to look for any inconsistencies or typical scam language. They also check ads by location and flag anything originating from a country we know to be the source of attempted scam listings (Nigeria is the most common – it has been estimated that the Nigerian scam industry is second only to its oil industry in terms of revenue created). The filters then quarantine any dubious ads and we sort through them manually to check they're okay (which by far the majority are) before letting them onto the site.

We also check all the photos and videos uploaded and weed out any which are either unsuitable (we had one particularly 'intimate' video submitted a couple of years ago – I'll leave the rest up to your imagination – Rupert) or contain direct contact information. Which leads us on to . . .

Keeping your email address safe

Many classified listings sites publish your contact details directly onscreen for anyone to see. SpareRoom don't do this for a couple of reasons.

Firstly, displaying your address directly on the advert allows automated software to scan the page, copy your email address and add it to a mailing list, resulting in you getting loads of spam emails. This process, known as 'email harvesting' or 'trawling', goes on undetected all the time and is one of the major ways spammers get your contact details so they can offer you Viagra and breast implants.

Secondly, only allowing registered users to contact you through the site makes everyone subject to our anti-scam checks. This doesn't mean we check up on everyone using the site (with over a million users we'd never manage it anyway), just that we check any messages flagged by our filters as suspicious. It also means that if a scam advert does make it onto the site (it does happen occasionally) we can see who has received messages from the fraudulent user and warn them.

Rupert says:

'In ten years of running flatshare sites, we've come across most of the ways people use to try and con unsuspecting members of the public. Some of them seem so ludicrously obvious to us now that we wonder why anyone falls for them (although someone, somewhere must, or the scammers wouldn't persist), others can be subtle and far more difficult to spot. That's why we employ several methods of quarantining suspect ads (both manual and automated) so we can check them before they get as far as our users. We can't vouch that everyone who advertises with us will make a great flatmate but we can ensure that, as far as is humanly possible, we protect you from anyone intent on defrauding our users.'

General security tips

The first golden rule in dealing with anything involving large amounts of money is IF IT SEEMS TOO GOOD A DEAL TO BE TRUE, IT PROBABLY IS.

Most successful scams play on our desire to either get something for nothing or get a great deal on a transaction. When it comes to renting rooms, if something looks amazing and is much cheaper than other rooms in the area then exercise caution. By all means contact the advertiser but maintain a healthy level of scepticism.

> **Rupert says:**
> 'Don't forget, all ads on SpareRoom have a "report this ad" link. If you think something looks dodgy then let us know and we'll have a look at it for you. We spend hours each week looking at fake or suspect ads so we'll be better at spotting them than you. It's all part of the service so don't think you can't get in touch if in doubt.'

In addition, there are a few general rules you can follow to make sure your room or flatmate hunting experience is a safe one.

DON'T PART WITH ANY CASH UNTIL YOU'VE SEEN THE ROOM

If you're looking for a room, you should never hand over any money or sign a contract until you've seen the property. However plausible the reasons you can't see it today may seem, hold off – if the landlord is genuine they won't mind and will understand your caution.

Similarly, if you're renting out a room, don't let someone take it unless they've been to see it (or, at the very least, met you in person). Remember, if you're renting out a room or taking in a lodger and need a little more peace of mind, you can always perform a few standard security checks before you sign the contracts.

SpareRoom offers a tenant referencing service, which you can access via www.SpareRoom.co.uk/content/info-landlords/tenant-referencing.

EMAIL ADDRESSES ARE NOT PROOF OF IDENTITY

If your prospective flatmate, tenant or lodger conducts all their correspondence by email, you shouldn't take their email address as sole proof of identity. Most free email addresses (Yahoo, Hotmail and the like) don't require any form of ID to sign up for so are easy to set up and use. Obviously if the person you're dealing with has a (functioning) work email address with a recognized company or organization, then you have a bit more security in terms of knowing where they work. You should always get a telephone number as well as an email address though.

BE WARY OF 070 NUMBERS

Phone numbers beginning 070 may look like UK mobile numbers but can, in fact, be routed to almost any number in the world. There are legitimate uses for these numbers (the user may not want their personal number appearing in an advert for example) so don't assume they're suspect, just make sure that anyone you intend to move in with gives you a landline or UK mobile number too. If they're genuine and the 070 number was just for their own security then they'll be fine with this.

DON'T PRESUME, IF YOU'RE NOT SURE THEN ASK

If you are unsure at any point in your dealings with someone, then ask for clarification. Any genuine landlord, flatmate or agent will be happy to answer questions. The golden rule is always 'if it seems too good a deal to be true, it usually is'.

DON'T LEAVE SENSITIVE DOCUMENTS LYING AROUND

If you're conducting viewings for a new lodger or flatmate, then make sure you don't leave any bank statements, cheque books, passports or other sensitive documents lying around in full view. This may seem like being over cautious (and in most instances that will be true), but why take the risk?

FEEL SAFE

If you're worried about heading off to viewings in areas you don't know (particularly late at night), you can always take a friend with you. Failing that at least let someone know where you're going and tell them you'll give them a quick call to let them know when you're done and on your way back (if you do this make sure you do call).

DON'T USE WESTERN UNION TO SEND MONEY

If a landlord asks you to send your rent and deposit via Western Union be extremely cautious, especially if the landlord lives overseas. Western Union payments are untraceable so there's not much you can do if someone takes your money and does a runner. Western Union is fine for sending money to friends and family (which is what most people use it for) but it's not suited for other transactions like paying rent so avoid it wherever you can.

ALWAYS GET A RECEIPT

If you're paying money to a landlord, agent or flatmate for rent or a deposit, make sure you get a receipt. If you pay by bank transfer or cheque then you've got a record of the transaction but otherwise get it in writing. Your landlord shouldn't mind doing this (and agents should expect it) – if you're paying money for a tenancy, you have a right to a receipt of your payments.

BEWARE ANYONE OFFERING TO OVERPAY YOU FOR ANYTHING

By far the most common form of online scam is the one known as the 'overpayment scam'. You don't need to know all the details – simply put, if anyone offers to pay you over the odds (usually by cheque) and asks you refund the balance, then walk away. The scam uses fake or stolen cheques and works on the perception that cheques clear in a few days when, in fact, they don't finally clear until the issuing bank has got the cheque back. By paying any money back you're giving your own cash away as the original cheque will be cancelled.

If you're interested in how this and other online scams work, or would like a little more information on online security go to: http://netcred. co.uk/security.

ALWAYS EXPECT A CONTRACT

If you see a room you like and the landlord or agent lets you take it without a contract of any kind, stop and think before handing over any money. If there's no contract, you have no legal right to be there and very little in the way of other rights. A contract will protect you as well as your landlord, so don't presume that no contract is good news.

If you pay your rent by standing order or cheque then you'll have a record you've paid money to the landlord, which suggests some form of verbal agreement at the very least. This should be enough, in the event of any dispute, to prove that you are a tenant but a clear contract will make things much easier if anything does go wrong.

KEY POINTS TO REMEMBER

- Never send money to anyone using Western Union unless you know them and trust them absolutely.

- If something appears to good to be true, then it probably is.
- Never agree to take a room until you've seen it.
- Don't let anyone take your room who hasn't been to see it or met you in person first.
- Get a receipt for any money you hand over.
- If you're showing someone around your flat don't leave sensitive documents out.
- Take someone with you or let them know where you're going (particularly late at night).

For more information on online security, go to: http://netcred.co.uk/security.

Useful Resources and Links

We've put any useful resources and links into the relevant chapters but, as a quick reference guide, they're listed here as well so you can find what you need in a hurry, without having to remember which chapter you saw it in. We've also put any relevant content you may want to print out and use (such as checklists and sets of questions) in a special micro-site for this book, which you can find at: www.SpareRoom.co.uk/essentialguide.

Flatshare and related sites

www.SpareRoom.co.uk
www.intoLondon.com
www.speedflatmating.co.uk
www.findaflat.com

Information and advice

www.Direct.gov.uk
www.cccs.co.uk
www.adviceguide.org.uk
http://england.shelter.org.uk
http://scotland.shelter.org.uk/home
www.lodgers.com
www.HMO.org.uk
www.tvlicensing.co.uk
http://netcred.co.uk/security

Useful tools

Budget calculator:
http:/www.yourmoney.moneyadviceservice.org.uk/tools/budget_planner.html

Postcode list:
www.listmasters.co.uk/postcodes.php

Housemate compatibility test:
http://www.housemateheaven.com/lifestyles.php

Find a Gas Safe Register accredited installer:
www.gassaferegister.co.uk

Tenant referencing:
www.SpareRoom.co.uk/content/info-landlords/tenant-referencing

Bill calculator and finance organizer:
www.ioweyou.co.uk

Shelter local advice directory:
http://england.shelter.org.uk/get_advice/advice_services_directory

London links

www.intolondon.com/tubemap
http://journeyplanner.tfl.gov.uk
https://oyster.tfl.gov.uk/oyster
www.tfl.gov.uk/gettingaround/9442.aspx (guide to river services)
www.thetrainline.com
www.tfl.gov.uk/tfl/roadusers/cycling/maps/maps-and-guides.aspx
www.tfl.gov.uk/tfl/gettingaround/findaride/default.aspx
    (minicab finding service)
www.ncp.co.uk
www.tfl.gov.uk/home.aspx
www.tfl.gov.uk/roadusers/congestioncharging/default.aspx

Appendix: London Postcodes

Here's a quick reference guide to the postcodes you'll find in London flatshare ads. These cover London itself; as you venture further out you'll find some of the outlying areas have their own postcodes (such as Croydon – CR). For information on UK postcodes in general, and a list of what the prefixes stand for, go to: www.listmasters.co.uk/postcodes.php

EC

EC1	Aldersgate, Finsbury, Holborn
EC2	Bishopsgate, Cheapside
EC3	Aldgate
EC4	St. Paul's

E

E1	Whitechapel, Shoreditch
E2	Bethnal Green
E3	Bow
E4	Chingford
E5	Clapton, Homerton
E6	East Ham
E7	Forest Gate
E8	Dalston
E9	Homerton
E10	Leyton
E11	Leytonstone
E12	Manor Park
E13	Plaistow
E14	Poplar (Isle of Dogs)
E15	Stratford, West Ham

E16	Victoria Docks, North Woolwich
E17	Walthamstow
E18	South Woodford
E20	Walford (just kidding – this is the fictional postcode where the soap opera *Eastenders* is set)

NW

NW1	Regent's Park, St. Pancras
NW2	Cricklewood, Dollis Hill
NW3	Hampstead
NW4	Hendon
NW5	Kentish Town
NW6	Maida Vale, Kilburn
NW7	Mill Hill
NW8	St. John's Wood
NW9	Colindale
NW10	Willesden
NW11	Golders Green

SE

SE1	Borough, Waterloo
SE2	Abbey Wood
SE3	Blackheath
SE4	Brockley
SE5	Camberwell
SE6	Catford
SE7	Charlton
SE8	Deptford
SE9	Eltham
SE10	Greenwich
SE11	Kennington
SE12	Lee
SE13	Lewisham
SE14	New Cross
SE15	Peckham
SE16	Bermondsey, Rotherhithe
SE17	Walworth
SE18	Plumstead

SE19	Crystal Palace
SE20	Penge
SE21, SE22	Dulwich
SE23	Forest Hill
SE24	Herne Hill
SE25	Norwood
SE26	Sydenham
SE27	West Norwood
SE28	Thamesmead

WC

WC1	Bloomsbury, High Holborn
WC2	Strand, Holborn

W

W1	West End
W2	Bayswater, Paddington
W3	Acton
W4	Chiswick
W5	Ealing
W6	Hammersmith
W7	Hanwell
W8	Holland Park
W9	Maida Vale, Paddington
W10	North Kensington
W11	Notting Hill
W12	Shepherd's Bush
W13	West Ealing
W14	West Kensington

N

N1	Angel
N2	East Finchley
N3	Finchley
N4	Finsbury Park
N5	Highbury
N6	Highgate

N7	Holloway
N8	Hornsey, Crouch End
N9	Lower Edmonton
N10	Muswell Hill
N11	New Southgate
N12	North Finchley
N13	Palmers Green
N14	Southgate
N15	Stamford Hill, South Tottenham
N16	Stoke Newington
N17	Tottenham
N18	Upper Edmonton
N19	Upper Holloway

SW

SW1	Westminster, Victoria
SW2	Brixton
SW3	Chelsea
SW4	Clapham
SW5	Earl's Court, West Brompton
SW6	Fulham
SW7	South Kensington, Knightsbridge
SW8	South Lambeth
SW9	Stockwell
SW10	West Brompton, Chelsea
SW11	Battersea
SW12	Balham
SW13	Barnes
SW14	Mortlake
SW15	Putney
SW16	Streatham
SW17	Tooting
SW18	West Wandsworth
SW19	Wimbledon

Index

admin fee, 31, 72, 123
advertising your room, 39-43
  photos, 42
  preparing the room, 42
  video, 42
agents, 72, 123, 137
app *see* iPhone app
assured shorthold tenancy, 6, 72, 124
  eviction, 132-3
assured tenancy, 73
  eviction, 133-4
AST *see* assured shorthold tenancy

bedsits, 10-11, 73
bills, 100, 110-21
  getting behind with, 119-21
  paying, 118-21
broadband, 17, 113
buddy ups, 28, 73
budget, 15-16, 20, 144
budget calculator, 16

choosing a flatmate, 22-5
cleaning, 24, 93-9, 128
conflict, 102-7
congestion charge, 157-8
contents insurance, 74
contracts, 31, 74, 122-7, 165
council tax, 75, 113-15
  lodgers, 57, 114
  students, 115

couples, 22-3, 35, 37-8
credit checks, 61, 75, 123

deposits, 31, 61-2, 74, 110, 127-9
eviction, 76, 131-4
  lodgers, 65-6, 133-4
  types of tenancy, 132-4

finding a flatmate
  how to look, 43
  placing an ad, 39-42
  where to look, 38-9
  who to live with, 34-8
finding a flatshare
  how to look, 27
  online, 26
  questionnaire, 25
  viewings, 30
  what to look for, 16-18
  where to live, 20-1
  where to look, 26
  who to live with, 22-3
food, 118
fractional letting, 77
  see also Monday-Friday lets
furniture, 31, 57, 62, 63

gas and electricity, 111-12
gas safety, 53, 60, 67
gender, 22, 36

harassment, 134-6
HMO (House in Multiple
    Occupation), 54, 78, 130-1
house rules, 24, 58, 105

insurance, 32, 56, 104-5
    and lodgers, 56
    landlord's, 79
    room contents, 56, 83, 116
inter-sharer agreement, 79, 125
inventory, 62, 79, 129-30
iPhone app, 30, 43

joint and several, 6, 79, 126

key meters, 79, 112

landlord
    living with, 7-9
    trouble contacting, 137
leaving notes, 104-5
live in landlord, 7, 80
living with a family, 47-8
lodger
    living as, 7
    preparing for a, 55-63
    providing meals for, 7, 47, 49, 51
lodgers
    benefits of taking in a, 52
    conflict, 65, 105-6
    contracts, 59, 126-7
    council tax, 57, 114
    credit checks, 61
    deposit, 53, 61-2
    eviction, 65-6, 133-4
    insurance, 56
    living with a family, 47-8
    placing an ad, 60
    tax, 46, 53, 63-4
    viewings, 60-1
    who can take in a, 51-6

London
    areas, 140-5
    budget, 144-5
    driving, 157-9
    finding accommodation, 139-44
    how to look for a room, 146-8
    postcodes, 150-1, 169-73
    public transport, 151-6
    safety, 149-50
    types of let, 148

Monday-Friday lets, 12-13, 41, 52,
    81, 148

noise, 99-100

online security, 26, 39, 160-6

parties, 99
partners, 59, 101
periodic tenancy, 82, 124
pets, 23, 36
phone, 113
postcodes, 21, 82, 150-1, 169-73
privacy, 100-2
professional flatshares, 9, 29
public transport, 20, 151-6

references, 82-3
Rent a Room Scheme, 7, 46, 53,
    63-4, 83
rent, paying, 108-10, 119
room contents insurance, 56, 83, 116
room shares, 11-12
room wanted ad, placing, 27-8

safety, 160-6
    online, 26, 39, 160-6
seasonal lettings, 84
setting up a flatshare, 33
size of property, 18-19

smokers, 23, 36
speed flatmating, 2, 28-9, 43, 85,
    147-8
sublets, 13-14, 85, 125

tenancy agreements, 84
  lodgers, 126-7
  re-signing fee, 123
  types of, 124-6
  whole property, 122
tenancy deposit scheme, 53, 85-6,
    110, 124, 128-9
tube line search, 27, 146

TV licence, 117-18

viewings
    finding a flatmate, 43-5
    finding a flatshare, 30-3
    interview notes, 45
    questions to ask, 30-3

water, 116
where to live, 20-1
who shares, 3
whole properties, 33
why share, 1